I0162430

"Wisdom That Transforms. Action That Lasts."

Our Commitment

We believe that true wisdom has the power to transform lives. Our mission is to equip readers with timeless insights and practical tools that inspire growth, guide decisions, and empower purposeful living. We don't just inform—we empower.

Our books combine profound understanding with real-life application, enabling readers to unlock their potential and navigate life's challenges with clarity and confidence. With each step guided by wisdom, we help you create lasting change and live the life you deserve.

When wisdom meets purpose, transformation follows.

Copyright

ISBN   978-1-952359-45-3   (paperback)
ISBN   978-1-952359-46-0   (ebook)

This book is available as an audiobook on our Amazon Life Planning book series page:	

"Practical Wisdom for Real-Life Challenges!

For More Information About the Life Planning Series:

www.lifeplanningtools.com

Life Planning Series
by J. S. Wellman

Choose Leadership

Be an effective leader.

J. S. Wellman

LIFE PLANNING SERIES
J.S. WELLMAN

Extra-mile Publishing

This book is available as an audiobook on our
Amazon Life Planning book series page:

Table of Contents

Message From the Author

Unlock Your Potential with Timeless Wisdom!

The general purpose of this book and the Life Planning Series is to encourage you to pursue actions and character traits that will produce your best life. The Series addresses ten different activities or traits that help people improve their lives, and *CHOOSE Core Values* addresses sixteen separate core values that you might consider beneficial.

Understand that you can improve or acquire high personal character and outstanding habits, no matter how good or bad your life may be at the moment. Good personal character and life habits can be achieved.

You don't have to read all the books in this series to make a significant change or improvement in your life. Find the books that focus on the areas of your life that you want to improve and dig in.

Know that this is a progressive journey. You don't need to climb the highest mountain immediately. You may just want to learn more about the basic principles and concepts. This Series and this book will provide you with a foundation for decisions relative to your lifestyle, goals, priorities, and commitments.

The key to developing high character and making good decisions in your life is *intentionality*. The Life Planning Series will help you identify the path you want to travel but you will need to be intentional about walking that path. If you want to make progress toward the goal of living a better life, you must intentionally take action.

Change will require making good decisions, establishing important core values in your life, setting priorities, and making commitments. This book will help you identify the values in life that will produce your goals and objectives. High personal character and good habits can be achieved if you want them.

This Series is designed to help you smooth out the path for your life journey. But, remember, all actions (both words and deeds) have consequences. These consequences will impact you and all those around you.

The key to your success is: "*Decide you want to do it and work at it regularly*."

Steve

"Set your mind on your future and commit to being the very best you can be!"
Stephen H Berkey[2]

"Wisdom to decide and the steps to succeed."

Free PDF
Living Wisely
The Life Planning Guide

A Quick-Start Guide to Purposeful Living and Wise Decisions!

Discover the five life domains: purpose, people, principles, productivity, and perspective. Wisdom is the ability to apply truth and logic to real-life decisions and produce good outcomes. It influences your choices and will produce action that lasts. Consider and apply the five practical wisdom principles for daily living. (6 pages)

Free PDF: https://getwisdompublishing.com/resource-registration/

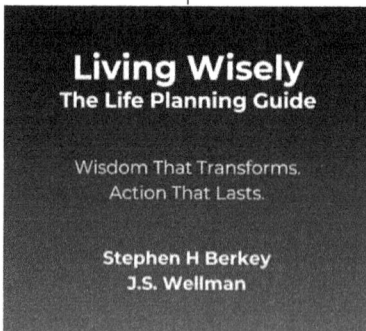

Living Wisely
The Life Planning Guide

Wisdom That Transforms.
Action That Lasts.

Stephen H Berkey
J.S. Wellman

Free PDF

Five Practical Principles For Life

When wisdom meets purpose, transformation follows.

Free PDF
Wise Decision-Making

[Get the ebook version for 99 cents]

You can make good choices.

This free resource provides a project-oriented perspective and gives ten detailed steps to analyze issues/problems to determine a solution. (26 pages)

Good decisions expand your horizons. Don't allow the fear of decision-making paralyze your ability to make good choices. Think through the reasonable alternatives and move forward. When your eyes are on the goal, making good decisions is easier.

Free PDF: https://getwisdompublishing.com/resource-registration/

Kindle ebook for 99 cents: https://www.amazon.com/dp/B09SYGWRVL/

Ebook

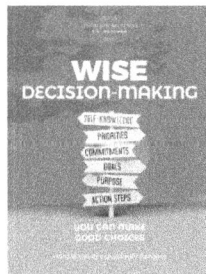

Free PDF

Make Thoughtful Decisions!

Good decisions expand your horizons.

The Life Planning Series
provides real-life tools
for wise decision-making
and personal transformation

Wisdom to Decide.
Steps to Succeed.
Life Starts Here!

Chapter 1 – Introduction

Life Planning Based on Wisdom!
Build Wisdom. Build Life!

We want to inform, encourage, and inspire you to choose character and improve your life.

The second and equally important purpose is to help you implement specific changes in your life.

Our third goal is to encourage you to pass it on. It is our desire that you will not only obtain this knowledge, but pass it on to others – particularly friends, children, grandchildren, or students.

An African proverb says, *"Don't spend all day rejoicing on your bench. When you pray, move your feet!"* The message of this proverb is that if you want to accomplish something, nothing will happen if you're sitting on your bench all day.

Growth and improvement, including living a better life, requires action and intentionality. The good news is that you can use the information in this book to acquire knowledge that will help you follow a path to a better life.

Those who want to develop a *total life plan* can do that by acquiring our *Life Planning Handbook*. We will discuss that book later in this chapter.

WHY READ THIS BOOK

The ideal reader of this book is someone who wants to accomplish any of the following:

- learn more about this subject,
- improve your life circumstances,
- live a better life with less stress,
- dig more deeply into the meaning of this subject and how it might impact your life,
- overcome the chaos of life, family or work relationships, or
- learn how to make good or better decisions.

PERSONAL GROWTH

We encourage you to make good choices and improve your personal and family life. This process is often referred to as personal growth or personal development. There are many good reasons for pursuing personal growth in your life:

- to find personal peace, meaning, and purpose,
- to gain more control over life situations,
- to acquire certain skills or abilities,
- to become more disciplined,
- to improve or overcome negative attitudes,
- to expand your horizons,
- to make better decisions,
- to open new avenues of understanding, or
- to change certain outcomes in your life.

It is our hope that this book will help you identify conditions in your life you would like to improve. You may need only some help focusing on the right things. You may just want guidance in finding things you can tweak to make a few changes in your lifestyle. You may want a clearer vision of your goals. Or you may want to do some serious work on some particular aspect of your life. Our Life Planning Series will help you achieve any of these goals and desires.

About *CHOOSE Leadership*

Great leaders aren't born—they are developed. What if you could become the kind of leader people trust, follow, and admire—starting today?

Whether you're leading a team, managing a project, or simply want to elevate your influence, *Choose Leadership* shows you how to unlock your leadership potential and make a lasting impact. This book equips you with the practical tools, mindset shifts, and core character traits you need to rise to the challenge—no matter your starting point.

You'll discover how to:

- Build trust and credibility through integrity and follow-through
- Communicate clearly, confidently, and persuasively
- Motivate and inspire others with purpose-driven leadership
- Navigate change and solve problems with calm confidence
- Make wise decisions using a step-by-step framework
- Commit to excellence, learning, and long-term growth

Being a great leader isn't about having a title—it's about how you influence and empower others. This book helps you cultivate the habits, principles, and vision of someone who gets results and earns respect.

Whether you lead a team of five or fifty, or simply want to lead yourself better, this book will guide you toward the traits that define outstanding leadership. It's straightforward, actionable, and designed to help you grow both personally and professionally.

THE LIFE PLANNING SERIES

The Life Planning Series covers most of the important subjects that you would address in an attempt to live a good or better life. Most of the books address one particular subject, help you identify your life goals, and guide you in creating action plans to achieve those goals. One exception is the Life Planning Handbook which will help you develop a complete life plan.

The Series in total addresses such topics as integrity, choosing friends, guarding your speech, working with diligence, making sound financial decisions, having a positive self- image, leadership, faith, choosing core values, and love and family.

Core values of The Life Planning Series

The Life Planning books are developed around ten core values and principles:

1. Wise sayings, parables, proverbs, common sense, and street smarts provide an underlying foundation for gaining knowledge, understanding, and wisdom.

2. Honesty, integrity, and living a life based on truth are the foundational character traits for achieving a life of hope and contentment. They are the cornerstones to living a better life.

3. There are five Primary Life Principles:

- be honest, live with integrity, and base your life on truth,
- choose your friends wisely,
- choose your words carefully,
- be a diligent and hard worker, and
- make sound financial choices.

4. Life change is possible. You can make positive changes and expect good results to follow, but all choices have consequences.

5. It is not necessary to change a large number of character traits in order to achieve significant life improvement. Changing a few *key* areas can have a major impact on your quality of life.

6. The key to making any life change is *intentionality*.

7. Perfection is not possible, but if you aim for it, you can achieve significant results. Nothing will be attained if you do not try.

8. We will be open about the difficulties, barriers, and walls that you might experience in implementing life change. Understand that barriers can be torn down.

9. The ultimate purpose in this series is to develop an effective plan for improving life circumstances. It is not our intent to provide lengthy textbooks on the particular subjects. Our presentation of the text material will be limited to what you need to know in order to develop an effective plan to improve your life.

10. Life is a progressive journey requiring good choices and a solid foundation for the future. Time is needed to implement change. Patience and perseverance will be necessary to achieve the desired results.

Transform Your thinking. Transform Your Life!

THE BOOKS

Go to the Life Planning Series page
to choose the book you want:

https://www.amazon.com/dp/B09TH9SYC4

THE LIFE PLANNING HANDBOOK

This is a unique book in the Life Planning Series. The purpose is to produce a total and complete *Life Plan* for your life. The sections include:

1. Life Principles and Character Attributes
2. Habits
3. Friends and Family Relationships
4. Work and Work Ethic
5. Education
6. Community Service
7. Money and Wealth
8. Health
9. Spiritual

The planning process in the Handbook will examine your skills and abilities, your personal life values, priorities, and commitments. The book will help you identify your life goals and create action steps to achieve those goals.

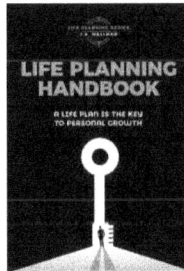

This book will generate purpose, direction, and growth in your life.

Go to https://www.amazon.com/dp/1952359325
to get your copy now.

Chapter 2
Consequences

"Mess with the bull and
one usually gets the horns."
Latin American saying[3]

GENERAL

Consequences are a vital concept in our understanding of making good choices and setting goals to have a successful life. Thus, this chapter on consequences will appear in most of the books in the Life Planning Series.

You have complete freedom to choose what you want to do, but you cannot choose the consequences. Thus, poor choices can be a disaster. We bear the consequences of our words and actions. It is like a law of nature.

Consider the manager who prioritizes titles and recognition over trust and service. His team disengages and productivity drops. Only after he begins listening, supporting others, and aligning his leadership with shared goals does morale and momentum return. Leadership isn't about position—it's about influence rooted in trust and purpose.

If you don't want to suffer the negative results of poor decisions, think in advance what your actions are likely to produce. What you do and what you say will have lasting impact on yourself and on others.

THERE WILL BE CONSEQUENCES

Life is a series of decisions and choices. We are constantly making choices about both significant and insignificant things. Choices shape the course of our lives. Some people learn a great deal from the consequences of their actions and others seem oblivious.

For example a team can fall apart under a self-serving leader who ignores feedback and seeks blame. But when a new leader steps in with a servant mindset, uplifting others and putting the mission first, performance can be restored. When leaders lead by serving, they don't just get better results, they build people who can multiply those results.

Physical consequences are a law of nature. If you touch a hot stove you will get burned. If you walk into the street in front of a truck you will be injured. Behaviors have predictable consequences as well. If you cheat and lie, people will stop doing business with you and your reputation will suffer. If you are not dependable, people will no longer trust you.

By definition consequences occur as a result of something else happening. The result may occur immediately or it could take a while, even years. This is often one of the reasons that we make poor choices – the consequence does not occur immediately and because of this we think there will never be consequences.

The actual consequences you experience will vary depending on your circumstances, but there will be consequences nonetheless. The degree or size of the consequence will also vary, but we should not be fooled into thinking small transgressions have no consequences.

*"One who steals has no right
to complain if he is robbed."*
Aesop[4]

THE FARMER AND THE OX

There was a farmer who had been plowing hard for many days with an ox and mule yoked together. The ox told the mule that they should pretend to be sick and rest. The mule declined saying, "No, we must get the work done, for the season is short." But the ox played sick and the farmer brought him hay and corn and made him comfortable.

When the mule came in from plowing the ox asked how things had gone. The mule said, "We didn't get as much done but we did okay, I guess." The ox asked, "Did the old man say anything about me?" Nothing," said the mule. The next day the ox played sick again. When the tired mule came in he asked again how it went. "All right, but we sure didn't get much done." The ox asked, "What did the old man say about me?" The mule replied, "Nothing directly to me, but he had a long talk with the butcher."[5]

This is similar to the message in the story concerning the consequences of a hearty breakfast to the chicken and the pig. A breakfast of ham and eggs to the chicken is a temporary inconvenience, but to the pig it is a permanent and lasting consequence – breakfast is a <u>real</u> commitment.

All actions have consequences!

COUNT THE COST

Someone has said that you will ultimately be invited to a party where you will dine on your own consequences.

Whether your actions were wise or unwise, you will eventually bear the consequences. Thus, it is important to think about the consequences in advance. What will result from your words or actions?

Regardless of the particular situation, it will always be easier to arrive at a positive outcome if you have thought ahead, evaluated the circumstances, and determined in advance how you will respond to the important challenges that arise in your life.

Remember an employee can model integrity, responsibility, and clear communication without being a formal leader with a title. Leadership isn't reserved for those in charge, it's a responsibility shared by everyone committed to doing their best work.

What you do and say in questionable circumstances will have a lasting impact on your life. Emblazon the following truth in your mind and on your heart:

Consequences shape lives.
Choices produce consequences
which direct the course of life.
Therefore, count the cost!

LEGACY

Our words and actions can have an impact for a long time. The ongoing impact of poor behavior is a concept that escapes many people. Poor decisions can affect a family for many generations. Bad behavior establishes a pattern that becomes the blueprint for a child's future behavior.

The experiences children have or observe become their normal responses in similar situations. What is witnessed by small children is later reproduced. They can learn to be trustworthy, reliable, and dependable, or they can learn to do drugs, smoke, and gossip. What a child sees modeled in the home becomes the normal response, and that behavior cycle can continue into many future generations.

If a parent avoids tough conversations, causing confusion and distrust, when they finally communicate honestly and listen with intention, the family will find direction and unity. Good parenting demands clear and open communication (leadership) because without it, even strong families can flounder.

Your legacy extends into future generations; therefore, be sure that it is a positive one! Most people have no concept of how their behavior can impact the future. This is dramatically demonstrated by comparing the lives of Jonathan Edwards and Max Jukes.

Jonathan Edwards was a Puritan preacher in the 1700s. His descendants demonstrate the powerful influence of wise choices and a godly life. At the turn of the 20th century, A. E. Winship decided to trace the descendants of Jonathan Edwards and compare them to a man known as Max Jukes.

Mr. Jukes was incarcerated in the New York prison system at the time Jonathan Edwards was preaching. Winship found that 42 of the men in the New York prison system could trace their heritage back to Max Jukes. Jukes, an atheist, lived a godless life. He married an ungodly woman, and from the descendants of this union 310 died as paupers, 150 were criminals, 7 were murderers, and more than half of the women were prostitutes.

In contrast, the record of Jonathan Edwards' progeny tells a much different story. An investigation of 1,394 known descendants of Jonathan Edwards revealed

- 13 college presidents,
- 65 college professors,
- 3 United States Senators,
- 30 judges,
- 100 lawyers,
- 60 physicians,
- 75 army and navy officers,
- 100 preachers and missionaries,
- 60 authors of prominence,
- 1 Vice-President of the United States,
- 80 public officials in other capacities,
- 295 college graduates.

Today, instead of the blessings like those that came to Jonathan Edwards' progeny, we are seeing a growing multitude like the descendants of Max Jukes! Have you seen a family in which the grandfather was an alcoholic – and his sons and grandsons abuse alcohol, too? Have you seen a family plagued with sickness, drug abuse, debt, or poverty? Often that is because someone in the past did not make good choices. We are going to leave a legacy for our children and grandchildren. Will we pass on a blessing or a curse?[8]

Your actions, both good and bad, establish the foundation of your life, lifestyle, and legacy.

We reap what we sow

In a number of his proverbs, King Solomon suggests that doing what is right is to be preferred over evil. King Solomon was known world-wide for his great wisdom. He wrote many proverbs recognized for their practical insight and wisdom. He describes the nature of righteousness as being immovable and that it will stand above evil.

Is your desire for doing what is "right" rooted deeply or is it planted in shallow soil that can easily be washed away? Solomon indicated that the wicked would ultimately be overthrown and that the righteous would survive because their character had roots that were deep and impossible to dislodge.

Solomon argued that it is better to be on the side of the righteous. The reasoning is the same as the man who chooses to build his house, business, or life on rock versus sand. If we build on sand (questionable ways) then our hopes and plans will never stand up against the storms of life. If we build on rock (high character) our plans should hold firm.

We do reap what we sow and if we sow badly because we have rejected what is right, the wise counsel of friends, or ethical core values, we will reap the negative consequences. Those who think they know everything frequently reject wisdom and follow their own plans and schemes. It has been said that those who insist on following their poorly chosen ways will often end up choking on them.

Lysa Terkeurst in her book, *The Best Yes,* says this about making decisions: "The decision you make determines the schedule you keep. The schedule you keep determines the life you live. And how you live your life determines how you spend your soul."

Think about that statement. You could say this truth in a number of ways – Ms. Terkeurst chose this particular description. But any way you say it the meaning is, *your decisions determine your life*. The consequences of your decisions constitute your day and your future. You are always living in the midst of the choices you make; therefore, make good choices. The consequences will determine how you live your life, or in Terkeurst's words, how you "spend your soul."

IT'S NOT FAIR

Unfortunately, life is not fair. Worrying about fairness, arguing about it, or fighting it will be of little value. Being "fair" generally means that everyone is treated equally (the concept of socialism). But life is not fair!
If you believe that life is intended to be fair, then it's not fair to others less fortunate that you were born in America and are therefore privileged. It is not fair that you have avoided poverty, wars, terrorism, natural disasters, tyrants, dying in an accident, abuse . . .

Obviously it is unrealistic to argue it's not fair that we experience the consequences of our own poor choices, especially since we are the ones making those poor choices. If we think we shouldn't incur the result of our poor choices then we certainly should not expect to experience the rewards of our good choices.

A toxic culture can take root where leaders tolerate corner-cutting and blame-shifting. But when values like integrity and accountability become non-negotiable, the organization rebuilds trust. A leader's personal values will ripple outward—what you allow sets the tone for what others follow.

Think about the consequences,
then choose wisely!

WHO TO BLAME

Blame is a big concern for many people today. When something bad happens, the first reaction by many is to find someone to blame. Many people no longer accept the concept of an "accident." It's become the cultural norm to assign blame and "make someone pay."

Some of us react in illogical ways to consequences. The most illogical is the person who totally ignores the obvious dangers of what they are about to do and then rather than accepting the consequences, casts blame. They become angry or embarrassed and attempt to find someone or something to blame in order to take the attention off their own poor judgment.

Taking responsibility for mistakes, misunderstandings, or accidents is becoming a lost art. Many children have been raised to believe they do not have to suffer consequences.

MISTAKES!

What happens when we make a mistake? A mistake is not the end of the world – it's a mistake, not a death sentence! If we make a wrong choice, we must rethink the issue and select another path. We all make mistakes. The real challenge in life is how we handle those mistakes.

Not every choice we make will be the right decision. Expect some failures in life and don't be overwhelmed if what you choose does not work out as you expect. If the choice was bad, wrong, or ill-advised, fix it!

A leader who chases quick wins and popularity will lose sight of the company's mission. In contrast, a leader who makes courageous, customer-focused decisions, even if unpopular, will earn long-term respect and have a positive impact. Leadership with backbone outlasts applause—it shapes the future.

> *Admitting mistakes and taking responsibility*
> *is a characteristic of those who*
> *are living their best life.*

BARRIERS

Difficulties and barriers can be overcome if you are determined to find a solution. It's a lot easier to make changes in life if you are receiving guidance and help. In addition to our books we suggest finding someone to join you in improving your life circumstances. If you cannot find someone to participate with you, find someone you can meet with weekly or periodically to discuss your progress, your difficulties, your needs, and most of all, your successes.

Here are some effective ways to overcome personal barriers:

1. Recognize that many barriers are in reality just excuses.
2. Recruit a support person (friend) to hold you accountable.
3. Recruit others to do it with you.
4. Recruit support from your family.

5. If time is a hurdle – work it out. Adjust your schedule and priorities.

Do not expect change, improvement, or miracles overnight. Ask for help when you need it.

> *"Being challenged in life is inevitable,*
> *being defeated is optional."*
> Roger Crawford[9]

TIPS TO AVOID UNINTENDED CONSEQUENCES

Here are five tips you could adopt before making decisions:

1. **THINK** before you act.
   Take time to consider the consequences.
   Ask yourself, "What would 'wisdom' do?"
   Think logically.

2. **LISTEN** to the advice of others.
   Seek out trusted friends.

3. **CONSIDER** the pros and cons.
   How will this decision impact me or others?
   Will I be proud of the outcome?
   What would my friends think?

4. **BE PATIENT**.
   "Sleep on it" is often excellent advice.
   Research as much as you can.

5. EMOTIONS often cause poor decisions.

Base your choices on facts and reality, not feelings.

Do not make decisions based on your emotions.

TIPS YOU COULD USE

a. Underline, circle, or highlight the tips above or anything in this chapter that you think could make the most impact if you implemented them in your life. You will revisit these choices at the end of the book in the Planning section.

b. There may be other things that you think would make a difference. Write them below:

_____

_____

_____

_____

"It is the peculiar quality of a fool to perceive the faults of others and to forget his own."

Cicero[10]

Chapter 3
The Leadership Life Principle

LIFE PRINCIPLE
Lead well and be a loyal follower.

"Leadership is influence:
nothing more, nothing less."
John Maxwell[11]

WHAT IS LEADERSHIP

If you do an internet search you can find almost any definition of leadership that fits your preconceived ideas about the subject. Here are several powerful quotes about leadership.

"Leaders instill in their people a hope
for success and a belief in themselves.
Positive leaders empower people
to accomplish their goals." Unknown[12]

"A good objective of leadership is to
help those who are doing poorly to
do well and to help those who are
doing well to do even better." Jim Rohn[13]

"The pessimist complains about the wind.
The optimist expects it to change.
The leader adjusts the sails." John Maxwell[14]

I've been in leadership positions most of my life. Some would say I was blessed and others might think I have been cursed. Regardless of how you might feel about leadership, one very simple definition for being a leader is: "*A leader is one who has followers.*"

This says nothing about how well you lead or where you are going, only that someone is following. If you have no one following, then you are not a leader. That does not mean you could not become one, but for the time in question, you are not leading anyone. If you are a leader, your words and actions are causing others to respond to you and work toward some common objective. Not necessarily a good objective, but a goal and common objective none-the-less.

Another interesting definition for a leader is: "One who is able to garner followers even though he treats his followers poorly." This type of leader is a Jekyll and Hyde type of individual. He has certain deficiencies (maybe many) in his leadership qualities and traits, yet there is something about him that draws people to his side or his cause. He may be very charismatic and people are drawn to his rhetoric and his style.

The problem with the Jekyll and Hyde type of leadership is that there may be little substance to the cause and followers are misled by a dynamic personality. Followers are often not drawn to the quality of the cause, but are attracted to the leadership style. Many businesses and causes have suffered badly at the hands of charismatic, but ruthless leaders.

There are other leaders who espouse bold action or unconventional behavior. They may even be controversial. People may be opposed to such leaders, but they are still leaders. They have followers and those followers may be totally committed to what the leader is doing, selling, or proposing.

A large group and its leaders may receive headlines and national attention, but many others are small groups. The size of the group is not relevant. If a group is working toward a common goal, like building a local park or senior center, they will have a leader.

Thus, leadership is not dependent on the number of followers or the nature of the goals. It simply means that there are people in general agreement with a desired outcome and they have come together to achieve that goal. This occurs in business, politics, the military, research, education, etc. Leaders are leading groups of all sizes in almost every avenue of life.

But leadership qualities are not necessarily common to everyone. Those blessed with natural abilities often find it much easier to achieve personal goals. Those without natural abilities must either work to develop leadership qualities or be satisfied with being a follower. Therefore, if you work in a manufacturing plant and do not have leadership or management abilities, you will most likely be working on the assembly line unless you have other valuable capabilities.

When we use the word leader or leadership in this book generally we mean the following:

> *Leadership is inspiring others to take*
> *action to achieve a common goal.*

THE LEADERSHIP LIFE PRINCIPLE

This book in the Life Planning Series is about leadership and the Life Principle is: ***Lead well and be a loyal follower.***

We believe that leadership is an important life principle in living a good life. Good leadership skills can elevate your lifestyle well above others who do not have such skills. Why? Leadership skills are much in demand by every type of organization.

If you have such skills, you can be assured of having a higher paying job. Leadership may be one of the most sought-after capabilities in the job market. One of the reasons that it is in such demand is that highly skilled leaders are difficult to find. There are certainly many who possess a number of the leadership skills, but few who are truly outstanding leaders.

Another factor is that leadership is needed in almost any job, project, cause, or group activity. Wherever there are a few people gathered together for a common cause, someone will emerge as a leader. That person may not necessarily be a good leader, but someone will begin to exercise the qualities and techniques of leadership in order that the task at hand gets completed.

Many students would be far better off if they went to college and studied how to become a leader, rather than obtain a general degree. The principles of leadership apply to any kind of work and activity. Similarly college students would be better off learning how to make sound decisions, solve problems, perform analytical thinking, apply logic, and gain wisdom, rather than waste their time in courses that will probably mean relatively little in their life or in the job market.

You may think I am being a bit harsh on education. If this were 1980 I would agree. But this is 2022 and the need for the typical college education has changed dramatically. Students need to learn how to think as well as possess other practical skills that are not being taught by most colleges or universities.

Do not misunderstand. If your college education is directly aimed at a skilled career like medical, engineering, accounting, nursing, etc. then going to school makes sense. But today there is relatively little value in a general education, particularly in light of the cost and the slim likelihood it will be beneficial in landing a great job.

SERVANT LEADERS

Great leaders are servant leaders. They lead not for themselves but for the benefit of their followers and the organization.

Servant leaders are humble and will put the needs of others above their own. Leaders who are prideful, aggressive, manipulative, selfish, or dishonest should be carefully evaluated and investigated before you place trust in their words. Persuasive words that are not matched by similar actions should be a red flag for followers.

Followers should not be misled by charismatic leaders whose cause is personal gain. A close look at the words and actions of charismatic leaders and speakers will reveal the nature of their motives. If the message is too good to be true, demands responses that border on servitude, requires you to believe or perform acts that are questionable, or even unlawful, then you must step back and carefully examine why you would follow or believe this leader.

Servant leaders have high personal character and good moral judgment, and they take responsibility for their actions. Some have said that modern politics and business are more in danger from the stench within than from competitive external threats or dangers. Thus, a nation or business can be in more danger from the actions of poor or evil internal leaders than from foreign nations or outside competitors.

Leadership skills and qualities can be used to achieve good or they can produce destruction. If you are a follower, you need to evaluate the character of your leader. Where are you headed? Is that where you want to be going? Who is holding the leader accountable? Do you trust the leader? Where are his loyalties?

> *"If your actions inspire others to*
> *dream more, learn more, do more, and*
> *become more, you are a leader."*
> John Quincy Adams[15]

ESSENTIAL LEADERSHIP QUALITIES

Leadership is a foundational skill that must be continually honed in order to achieve desired results. Many writers on the subject of leadership will list the ten (or 5 to 15) most important traits or skills required for individuals to possess in order to be an _outstanding_ leader. These traits may be identified by other writers as just the necessary qualities of any leader.

Our conclusion for these seemingly confusing or conflicting positions is that in order to be an excellent leader you must do the basics very well. Often the basic leadership skills are intertwined in many of the lists of principles or traits of leadership that are identified as being the most important.

Many of the key leadership principles, qualities, and traits are interrelated. Often you cannot have one without another. For example, good communication is a critically important quality. Communication must be clear, concise, open, and timely. Many of the principles of good leadership inherently require good communication. But "communication" is also a stand- alone quality.

For example, building relationships, inspiring others, and managing change all require good communication. In fact, if communication is not done well, it is likely that the trait itself will also not be very effective.

Thus you may notice throughout this book that some of the leadership traits are mentioned in more than one section or category. That's because many of the important leadership principles and qualities are very closely related and must be melded together to produce an outstanding leader.

Therefore, we are not sure how meaningful it is to identify a few _key_ qualities of leadership. But it is certainly important to identify all the _important traits_ and point out that any particular trait may not be more important than any other selected leadership trait.

We believe that most of the basic traits or qualities must be done well if you want to be a _good_ leader.

Although it may not be worthwhile to choose just three or four traits and say that if done well you can be a great leader, we will suggest that _communication_ might be the number one skill that is most critical for a leader because it impacts so many other leadership traits. Poor communication can cause other traits to be ineffective and derail any hope of being an outstanding leader.

THE KEY TRAITS

We believe that the following qualities or traits are necessary for anyone wanting to *excel* as a leader. We have numbered them for convenience only. We have also identified where that trait is more fully discussed in the book.

1. Effective communication (Principle #1).
2. Good problem-solving skills (Principle #3).
3. Commitment to organization (Principles #8, #11).
4. Commitment to employee training (Principle #2).
5. Commitment to excellence (Chapter 7, and Principle #3).
6. Ability to inspire and motivate others (Principles #6, #7, and #12).
7. Ability to manage change (Principles #5, and #9).
8. Personal character (Chapter 6 and Principle #4).

Most leaders in your organization will possess all these traits, some stronger than others. Lack of any one of these traits could create real leadership weakness. But if you want to *excel*, you must have them all and to a significant degree. Obviously having many of the other qualities and principals of leadership will strengthen your ability to be an outstanding leader.

You might notice that effective listening, self-discipline, and self-motivation are not included above. We think these are very important qualities but are inherently included in the eight traits above. We have also provided additional information on self-discipline in Appendix A.

Leaders should look for these traits when they are seeking to hire new people on their team. If you are hiring leaders, you should certainly be making some of these qualities absolute job requirements. If you are looking to advance people within your organization, you should also be looking for these traits.

Does this mean that all organizations should adopt all of these traits for their company? No, not necessarily! The traits and principles that drive your organization should be determined by the desires of the owners, the nature of the organization, and the industry. You must adapt your skills to the requirements of your organization.

SPECIAL NOTE: Pronouns

In today's culture it is recognized that great leaders may be either male or female. We have tried to reflect that truth by using the pronouns "him" and "her" interchangeably.

Wisdom to Action Challenge

Identify one person you influence (e.g., colleague, family member, mentee). Without invoking your title or authority, serve them in a way that addresses their growth or a shared goal. Reflect: How did this act of servant leadership deepen trust or inspire action?

Chapter 4
Leadership Principles

*"Real leadership...comes from realizing that
the time has come to move beyond waiting to doing."*
Madeleine Albright[16]

WHY LEADERSHIP PRINCIPLES MATTER

Leadership principles matter because they establish the tone and environment for the organization. If the organization is going to operate by the seat of someone's pants, these principles will be worthless because they will be ignored. Followers need to have confidence in their leadership. Leadership principles identify the characteristics of good leaders. Potential leaders who do not demonstrate these principles can be quickly identified as needing more training and development. Or, they may not be suited for leadership at all.

A leadership principle is a fundamental rule or established behavior or policy that is intended to be followed. It is intended to be an inherent part of something. Therefore, in a business organization these principles represent how the business is to operate and how people are to lead and represent the organization. Leadership principles assure that both the leadership style of the organization and the leaders themselves are founded on sound concepts and techniques. They will inherently direct leaders away from undesirable attributes and behavior.

If well-conceived leadership principles have been established, the organization can more accurately assess and measure performance. One cannot be held accountable for something that has not been clearly communicated. Thus, leadership principles are often part of the written operational procedures of an organization.

Why do good organizations make a big deal out of leadership standards? Simply because they provide controls and a framework for doing business that will, in the opinion of the organization, provide the best opportunity for success in their business. If leadership principles were not important they would not exist. But successful companies have demonstrated that establishing these principles is beneficial and will give an organization the best chance for success.

These principles inherently define what an organization values. They indicate what is important to the organization and how it intends to operate. The goal is to create the best environment for leaders and employees in order to provide customers with the best possible products and services. If quality is not an important value, products and services will tend to be overpriced. If customer service is not valued, customers will be frustrated when dealing with the company.

Leadership principles apply to everyone in the organization because leadership is the responsibility of all employees or followers. This is true because everyone is a leader to some extent. No one, including the president or CEO, is exempt from these principles. Leaders lead by example. These principles begin at the top and extend throughout the organization clear down to the mail room.

These principles create an environment that allows the organization to successfully compete in the marketplace. But the principles also help form and strengthen the character and capabilities of individual people. Good people doing a good job produce good products that other people want to acquire.

Success may be defined differently by different people and particularly people at different levels within the organization. As one progresses up the management ladder within an organization the goals become broader. At the top there is far more interest in the bottom line and what is expected to occur over the next five to ten years for the organization. Many CEOs are totally focused on the future and only think about the current year when necessary.

We have chosen to discuss the following principles because we believe they are the most important. These are not in any particular order except for Principle #1 which we believe may be the most critical to overall leadership success.

PRINCIPLE #1: COMMUNICATE

A great leader must communicate effectively. Just communicating is not enough. Your communications must produce the desired result.

Clear, concise, and open communication is a necessity for good leadership. Without good communication, followers can be confused and misled. Frequent communication usually is a signal to followers that they are cared about and that their needs are important. Clear and concise communication can prevent misunderstandings.

Knowing what the leadership is thinking will help followers believe in and trust decisions that are being made. Open communication helps establish good ongoing dialogue between workers and management.

The leader must make sure his words clearly communicate his meaning and intent. It is important to allow followers to believe they are part of a team and doing something important to achieve common goals.

The leader is part of a cohesive team but he is the one with his hands on the wheel. The leader knows the goal and steers the team toward that goal with effective communication.

Good leaders do not waste time with their communications. They communicate the information that keeps everyone informed and allows subordinates to make better decisions. Superfluous communication is kept to a minimum.

If followers understand the purpose and goal of the organization, they can contribute more effectively to the work of the team. Followers have a great deal of skill. They can help make the work environment difficult or easy.

Good communication encourages followers to buy into the team goals. This allows them to participate in the success of the team and the organization. Both leaders and followers need to know the mission. Keeping everyone informed allows for their input and cooperation in achieving common goals.

Poor communication can cause frustration, implementing improper procedures, or apathetic responses. When leaders communicate clearly, the response and feedback will be far more helpful and focused on the necessary issues that must be addressed. Good communication goes both ways and often requires both leaders and subordinates to listen well.

Good leaders communicate with humility. Instructions that are given in harsh and demanding styles will normally not be effective. Verbal instructions should be concise and should often be followed by written confirmation to avoid misunderstanding.

In today's workplace it is also necessary to be aware of different cultures when communicating with people or other companies. It is particularly important if you are operating in a global marketplace. Words often have different meanings in different cultures, therefore, chose your words carefully in a diverse environment.

Good leaders encourage subordinates to offer feedback and suggestions. The best communication is two-way to maximize clarity and cooperation. Effective communication going both up and down the chain of command is often a key to achieving common goals.

Leaders must not only communicate about the work but they should cast a vision for their employees about the organization, its purpose, and where the team fits in the mission of the organization. Knowledge helps employees relate to their job and to the organization. Employees want to know what they are doing and how they contribute to the end result.

Leaders help team members know where they fit in the organization, their importance, and what the future might look like. Good leaders paint a realistic picture of the future in order to excite employees about their work. A compelling story teller can transport employees into a work environment and the organizational possibilities that will motivate employees to give their best to the team and to the organization.

Take care of your people,
and they will take care of you.

PRINCIPLE #2: TRAINING and DEVELOPMENT

Change.

All good leaders pursue ongoing education in order to improve their capabilities and those of their team. Education does not stop just because an individual has reached a certain level within the organization. Good leaders are often committed to learning in order to implement new or efficient methods and systems. New ideas and procedures do not daunt leaders who want to rise to the top.

Therefore, good leaders are constantly seeking to learn new things and new ways. They are aware of what is new in the marketplace and what skills must be learned or refined. Good leaders are on top of emerging trends and the technology that may be driving those trends. They are not fearful about learning new skills or improving existing capabilities. Their mindset is on the purpose and mission and what will advance the organization in the marketplace.

Curiosity will often drive leaders to explore innovations, particularly in a rapidly changing environment. Today's leaders must keep on top of changing technology or they can find themselves stuck with obsolete equipment, outdated technology, and decreasing profit potential. An organization that is not keenly aware of the changes in the marketplace can quickly find itself falling behind in a highly competitive market.

Good leaders set aside time on a regular basis to keep on top of the changes in their industry. They are never satisfied with the status quo. New ideas and concepts are always of interest. Improvement is a primary goal for both themselves and the organization.

Personal development and training becomes a priority in a rapidly changing environment. Employees want to feel that they are growing and improving. If people are not growing they may feel stunted in their job and may leave an organization because they see no hope for their future.

Good leaders are always
looking for new possibilities!

Leadership training.

Good leaders practice what they preach. Just as followers need to be trained, so do leaders. The training may come from books, conferences, podcasts, webinars, or practical experience. It might even involve going to school or taking night classes. Good leaders will model improving their skills by learning about new things, strategies, or trends.

The goal of the leader is to grow and develop leadership skills while demonstrating the importance and usefulness of ongoing education and training to subordinates. The leader wants to inspire employees or followers to better themselves in whatever methods of self-improvement that might be appropriate.

If you are going to require much of your followers you need to be the one to demonstrate the value of what you are proposing or requiring. Lead by example. Demonstrate the value of ongoing training and education through your own growth.

A word of caution here is important. It may be easy for a leader to participate in development training. That may not be true of all the followers or employees. Leaders must be cautious not to try to outdo their followers when participating together. Arrogance will be a real barrier to followers or subordinates. Some workers may progress slower than others.

In some leadership situations you may be asked to organize and direct people who have more ability than you at their specific trade or skill. Make sure as a leader that you have a working knowledge of what subordinates are doing. A bus driver doesn't need to be a great mechanic, but he needs to understand the concepts or principles of engines, how they sound, and generally how they work in order to communicate effectively with those trying to keep his bus in top working condition.

Leaders prepare their workers to take on new or different tasks. A good leader will know in advance if his team can accomplish the tasks assigned. If there is valid concern, that leader will probably more closely monitor work progress. The leader himself may become involved in some of the work and the planning at the team level.

Knowing the capabilities of a team is as important as knowing its deficiencies. Teams cannot accomplish results for which they have inadequate training and understanding. A good leader knows the capabilities of his team and will manage to those strengths and weaknesses.

Followers are not disposable goods that can easily be replaced. Therefore advancing the capabilities of followers will enhance not only the individuals but also the greater purpose of the team. The leader who does what is good for her followers will receive respect, honor, loyalty, and good-will from those followers.

Good leaders may never be satisfied.

Constant and continuous improvement is often the watchword of effective teams. Having a particular job approved or accepted does not mean that a good leader will be satisfied. Being acceptable can be a long way from being good or excellent. Both leaders and followers must be honest in assessing themselves and their work. Apathy will tell you that a result is within the required parameters; honestly may tell you that you fell short of excellence.

The best leaders and teams are constantly looking for ways to be better. Don't be looking for ways to finish and get paid; be looking for ways that your work is heralded as "second to none." Leaders and followers should continually look for ways to raise their performance bar.

Personal growth and development does not need to be sophisticated and overly complicated. There are three important things to know in designing development programs:

- the strengths and weakness of the individual should dictate the development plan,
- targeted work assignments can help subordinates grow, and
- the basic qualities of leadership that need to be developed.

Key experiences are one of the foundational elements in leadership development. There is nothing like live experience where the results really matter to help develop leadership qualities. If your work is stretching your capabilities, you are learning and growing. Struggling personally with real live difficult problems will increase your ability to solve problems – it is much more effective learning than reading about it in a book.

Beyond being focused on certain leadership qualities, having the experience of leading will strengthen most of the basic qualities of leadership:

- building personal relationships,
- managing change,
- being accountable and requiring accountability,
- communicating effectively,
- inspiring others, and
- problem-solving.

Personalized training and education.

It is important to recognize that team development is not the same for every member of the team. If someone is already good at delegating and organizing he certainly doesn't need to be sent to a class on that subject. Personal development and training should be designed to fit the needs of the individual team member.

Some training might be provided for all management people in the form of a total group conference or seminar, but the most effective personal development will be specifically designed for the individual. There are different skills needed at different levels of management. Training should be designed for the specific needs of the individual and the position he or she holds.

Hiring.

Organizations should attempt to hire the very best employees available. Leaders should hire people under them that are better than they are. Leaders will raise the performance level of the organization with every good hire and deserved promotion. Certain leaders may be particularly skilled at recognizing talent. They should be asked for their evaluations on new candidates whenever appropriate.

Strong leaders are the key to the success of any organization. Such leaders can be acquired from many sources, not all within the organization. Good leaders make every effort to train new leaders from their own organization, but they do not neglect looking outside the organization. This is true from the CEO down to frontline supervisors and managers. Leaders are critically important because they individually determine the degree of success of the organization.

Individual leaders should always have someone ready and available to step into their job. There are many situations where leaders may be gone for days, weeks, or even months. They can be sick, on special assignment, or take jobs in other companies. If you are good at leadership development, you can be assured that head hunters are looking to raid your staff.

Therefore, training, education, and leadership development is an ongoing and constant activity for organizations wanting to excel in the marketplace.

"Leadership and learning are indispensable to each other."
John F. Kennedy[17]

PRINCIPLE #3:
DECISION-MAKING and PROBLEM-SOLVING

Good leaders are decisive. They know how to make decisions and usually follow some form of recognized process in arriving at decisions. They never appear flustered or confused. They are confident in their decision-making because they take the necessary time to evaluate and analyze the available information.

Decisions must not be made with inadequate information. Decision-makers acquire all the *available* data and information (although it may not be everything that exists) and then make a decision. Most good decisions can be made if the decision-maker has 60-80% of the available information.

Decisions are normally not made by committee. Good leaders evaluate the facts, get input from others, if necessary, and then decide. A good leader will exude confidence in her decisions, knowing that if the decision is wrong she will see the warning signs and fix the problem.

There is usually no clear cut alternative that you know is 100 percent right, and you will never get 100 percent of the information necessary to make a decision. Good leaders recognize that any decision is temporary and can be modified at any time additional information becomes available indicating a change is necessary. They are prepared to move forward based on the information they have, knowing that delays and indecision are really a "do nothing" answer to the question of doing something.

Results and outcomes are always unknown in advance. Perfect decisions are almost impossible. Good business leaders become comfortable in the uncertainty and become experts in monitoring their critical decisions.

Problem-solving.

Good leaders work at being excellent problem-solvers. Roadblocks and difficulties are only temporary inconveniences. They will dig into problems with their followers until the problem is identified and fixed. This skill may come naturally or it may be the result of training and education.

In today's workplace leaders must be skilled at solving problems. They must be able to make the very best decisions possible. Thus, problem-solving skills are crucial to being a good decision-maker. But a leader who does not have these skills, or one whose skills are not the best, needs to have followers or associates that do.

Problem solving is important in all phases of your organization. Every important thing you do involves problem-solving to some degree. As the issues become more important or complicated so does the need for the ability to solve problems.

Good leaders are skilled at solving problems.

Be Decisive.

Being decisive is also a valuable skill and a characteristic of good leaders. It means that you make decisions in a reasonable amount of time. Your team is never on hold waiting for your decision. You are able to choose quickly the right alternative among various possibilities in order to achieve the desired result. When decisions are delayed until all the information can be obtained, it may be too late to be effective in the marketplace.

Sometime being decisive is only a matter of knowledge and intelligence. At other times real wisdom is required to make the right choice. Failure to act and make a decision can often be as bad as making the wrong decision. Evaluate your options carefully and make a decision. That does not mean that you should be careless in order to make a quick decision. But once the situation has been adequately investigated, make a decision.

When the issues are clear and obvious it is easy to be decisive. But often you are faced with questions that have no obvious answer and no obvious solution appears. This is where good leaders will stand out among their peers. The good leader makes decisions knowing that he may need to change or shift his focus if new data indicates a change is necessary.

Outcomes are never guaranteed regardless of the amount of information available. Good leaders are comfortable making decisions in a fluid environment and willing to change on a dime if that decision proves inadequate or wrong.

Leadership is often disruptive – it does not promote or encourage the status quo.

Make Good and Timely Decisions.

Good decisions are not the result of guessing or good luck. They come about because of hard work and sometimes intense study. Wisdom and understanding must be able to take knowledge and apply it to the situation at hand to develop good working solutions. New ideas and concepts always need to be investigated and evaluated.

Poor decision-making or ineffective thinking can bring an organization to its knees. Critical thinking, effective problem-solving, insightful planning, and excellent execution of plans must be the expected role of good leadership. Timely decisions are often the key to success, particularly during times of dramatic change.

For practical help making decisions, see Chapter 9.

PRINCIPLE #4: CORE VALUES

Although Core Values are a foundation for everyone, they are particularly important for leaders. Leaders must have core values that drive their work, moral standards, and reputation. Followers will generally share similar core values as the leader, but they will not necessarily be the same or held as strongly.

Similar values create harmony and reduce the likelihood of confusion over instructions and motives. Leaders are likely to hold followers to their standards, even to the point of asking people to leave if they cannot adhere to the leader's core values.

This allows the leader to lead by example, expecting followers to imitate and reflect the stated core values. These values create and maintain the culture of the group or company.

Leaders do not allow confusion about core values to linger or create divided loyalties. If there is a problem with expectations, the leader must address it immediately.

Leaders do not waiver on their values. A leader cannot allow core values to be ignored or put aside by followers. If that happens it will appear the leader has favorites and doesn't really adhere to his core values. This can destroy the cohesion of the group.

Good leaders will implement actions and policies that benefit the entire team. They may work individually with followers or they may teach and motivate groups. Good leaders want everyone to know their role and purpose. This allows the team to contribute far beyond just completing assigned tasks. Both leaders and followers need a common belief in similar core values.

A bad team usually means a bad leader.

This is a difficult concept for many leaders to understand and accept because they would rather believe problems or failures are the result of poor or inadequate followers.

One major problem for some leaders is that they accept poor or sub-standard performance. This usually means that the result is also substandard. Everyone, including the leader, must be held accountable for poor performance. Standards must be enforced. Excellence must be required and substandard work must be rejected. If not, the result will be some degree of failure, loss of contracts, personal jobs, and even companies. Quality work and excellence should be demanded as necessary job performance characteristics.

It is the leader's job to focus a team on the end result and to communicate knowledge of the ultimate purpose. If he fails to do this, the entire effort could be a waste of time. Followers who haven't figured out what it means to be on a winning team must be encouraged, trained, and inspired. That's the leader's responsibility.

The high performing leaders and teams are looking for ways to be the best.

PRINCIPLE #5: MANAGE CHANGE

The one sure dynamic in this world is change. It will not stop or disappear. If you think it will then you will likely be the one to disappear. Recognizing and managing change is a necessary part of being a good leader.

Understanding that the world is constantly changing will certainly impact your life and careers. Monitoring change is an absolute necessity if you expect any degree of success. Change requires constant adjustment, frequent detours, and sometimes even a major revamp of purpose and mission.

In today's world if you cannot manage change you will not survive long. Technology is expanding at such a fast pace that if you are not adjusting to changes in your industry you will find yourself always playing catch-up.

This world has no sympathy for people or organizations who fail to adapt and change.

Change is going to happen whether we want it or not. Therefore, good leaders do not fight change, but embrace it. They don't have time to grumble about change because they are figuring out how to make change work for them.

Change can be a slow process or it can happen in a matter of weeks when there is a major paradigm shift. The reality is that such change was probably coming for some time and nobody was paying attention.

Change can produce a number of good results:

- increased efficiency,
- more effectiveness,
- greater growth,
- high productivity, or
- greater profits.

Leaders with exceptional talent and above average foresight can often see change coming. They will be prepared to take advantage of change and use it to overcome their competition. Poor leaders see nothing and may resist the impact of change, finding it difficult to deal with in a dynamic and fluid environment. Being curious and innovative is a good trait for a leader in today's environment.

> *"Innovation distinguishes between*
> *a leader and a follower."*
> Steve Jobs[18]

Therefore, a major requirement for good leaders today is that they have adequate tech-savvy. If you do not understand the basics of today's technology, it is not likely you can rise to any significant leadership level. In most organizations technology is an absolute requirement for business success and even survival. Thus, leaders must understand how it works, what it does, and how it can be used to improve their business. Existing leaders who don't possess adequate knowledge and understanding will be in danger of losing their jobs or simply reaching a point in an organization where they can no longer expect advancement.

"Our future success is directly proportional to our ability to understand, adapt, and integrate new technology into our work."
Sukant Ratnakar[19]

Much is expected of leaders during a time of dynamic change. Leaders must be focused on market developments but they cannot forget the purpose and mission of their organization. A dynamic market place can place great stress on an organization. Good leaders will often rise to the occasion during challenging times like this.

The quality of leadership is often the difference between an organization overcoming change or being dragged down because of it.

PRINCIPLE #6: LEAD BY EXAMPLE

If you want to inspire your followers, get in the trenches with them. Followers will be impressed with and uplifted by the leader who joins them in accomplishing the work. Inspired leaders work as hard as their followers and demonstrate diligence, hard work, and a positive spirit.

The most productive teams often have leaders who are not afraid to work alongside their followers. They reflect in their work what they say in their talk. If a leader demonstrates a bad attitude, followers will usually follow suit. Leaders get what they give.

Good leaders do not manage from afar and have little interaction with the work or the workers. Good leaders are tuned in to their followers and know their successes as well as their problems. They will step in and assist when necessary. They will take time to explain and train. Leaders want to achieve the best possible result and if that means spending time in the trenches, they will do it.

Good leaders walk the talk. Their actions as well as their words demonstrate their interest and involvement. The character and value of a good leader is frequently on display, not hidden behind a big desk or high walls.

Actions speak much louder than words. Followers can see through speeches that mean nothing to the leader. A real leader earns trust and respect because he is engaged with the work. A leader's true character is demonstrated in what he does and not in what he says. Followers will quickly ignore the words of leaders that are not consistent with their corresponding actions or the purpose and mission of the organization.

Leaders demonstrate respect in the way they act toward workers. Leaders who lead by bluster and harsh words are quickly ignored and usually inspire only the minimum work and cooperation. Of course, that leads to more loud words, and the cycle continues.

If you want good communications, then you must set the example. If you want an open atmosphere where all important issues are eligible for discussion, then you must be open to such. Secrets and topics that are off limits will not encourage an open and trusting environment.

Leading by example means the leader models the behavior she desires. If a leader wants respect then she must model courtesy, kindness, and encouragement. There are many ways to model the behavior you expect: be punctual, respect an employee's time, be an encourager, demonstrate kindness, dress appropriately, give credit to others for their work, be a good listener, etc.

Good leaders back up their words with actions that demonstrate character and respect. Leaders do not have to be friends with their followers, but they do have to earn their respect and loyalty. Good leaders do not have to spend time making grand gestures intended to demonstrate their leadership ability; they must simply lead well. Good leaders are committed to the goals of the project and the company. Their actions and practices should encourage workers to share the same commitment.

PRINCIPLE #7: TEAMWORK

It is sometimes said that teamwork is the key to a successful project or workforce. If workers are constantly competing to survive in their jobs, problems are likely to arise. A good leader wants everyone on the same page working toward the same goal, and not worrying about their jobs or being afraid to communicate with other people on the team or in the organization.

The best teams work together to accomplish a common goal. The best environment is one where the workers enjoy the work and have fun working together. They look forward to returning to work on Monday mornings. Good leaders encourage strong relationships among their workers in order to promote team building and collaboration.

All elements in a team and organization should cooperate and work together. If they don't, it is usually the leader's fault. Leaders must continually be on the lookout for possible problems that might create obstacles, animosity, or blame. The blame game will create friction and erect walls within a group. The leader must continually sell and promote teamwork toward the purpose, vision, or mission. Every member of a group is important and the leader must marshal the cooperation of all toward the ultimate objective.

If there is a weak link the leader must deal with it honestly and fairly. A leader cannot allow a team to fail because someone has been given responsibilities they cannot handle. The result could be chaos if the issues are not resolved. If a project fails the entire team will suffer.

If the problems are between different teams, the leaders of those teams need to assure subordinates that ways can be found to make the situation work. Teams must cooperate and help each other succeed. Remember, the mission of the organization is the controlling factor. Achieving the company mission is the overriding objective. All teams and team members need to support that overall goal.

An important responsibility of the leader is employing workers to utilize their capabilities. Teamwork problems tend to develop when workers are in jobs they can't handle or when they are so overqualified they are bored.

Train your followers as a team and match
their capabilities to their responsibilities.

PRINCIPLE #8: TAKING OWNERSHIP AND RESPONSIBILITY

Good leaders act like owners. Nothing is beyond their interest. Everything is important because they want the organization to succeed. They will work tirelessly to accomplish the mission of the company. They inherently take on the responsibility of an owner. They tend to think of themselves as ambassadors of the brand or the organization.

Good leaders will take on the task of fixing a problem even when the issue is not directly part of their work responsibilities. They will often tell their followers, "If you see a problem, fix it." You might hear that same leader say, "Don't assume somebody else is going to fix the problem. If you see it, fix it."

This mindset comes from the common perception that the company purpose and mission take precedence over all else and it is everyone's responsibility to work for the success of the organization. Thus, when a good leader sees a problem, he automatically takes ownership of the problem and will get it resolved. He would consider it a personal failure to ignore the problem simply because it's not really his area of responsibility. Obviously that doesn't mean he would intrude on the responsibilities of other team leaders.

A good leader feels ultimately responsible and he will do whatever is needed to successfully accomplish the goals of the team and the company. If the team is not performing, the leader will find and diagnose the problem, develop tactical or strategic solutions, obtain approval from management, and execute a solution. This may require hiring or firing, training and personal development, purchasing equipment, etc.

Unfortunately, the leader must also take responsibility for failures. A good leader will be forthright about problems, accept responsibility, and suggest possible solutions for the future. It is not easy for a leader to take such responsibility, but it is often in these failures that leaders grow the most.

It's like the quarterback in the NFL who takes the hit for his team when they lose. The quarterback may have played a great game, but he will take ownership of a loss, just like the leader will take responsibility for the mistakes of his team. Good leaders generally give credit to the team when success is achieved, rather than accept the accolades themselves. Leaders of this nature are admired and in great demand.

Good leaders are not afraid to make mistakes and when they make one, will take responsibility. It's okay to make mistakes. The problem is when mistakes are repeated because nothing was learned when the mistakes were first made. Good leaders take responsibility for their actions and conversely they will give credit and recognition to team members for work well done.

When the leader admits a mistake to the team, it empowers others on the team to take risks. Both life and work require risk-taking. If the world does not end when a mistake is admitted, followers feel free to challenge their own capabilities and take reasonable risks when the reward is worth it.

Leaders who admit mistakes gain the respect and loyalty of their team. It is much easier to relate to a leader who is real and genuine than one who considers himself beyond reproach. When mistakes are admitted they can be fixed and operations can move ahead without missing a beat.

Admitting mistakes also creates an atmosphere in which the focus is on fixing problems rather than on casting blame.

Take personal responsibility for leading.

No one will be impressed with your leadership just because you happen to sit in the corner office and have a view. You must have leadership qualities and display them to subordinates.

People follow and are loyal to good leaders. The organization's vision can cement the relationship between leaders and followers. But if the followers do not respect the leader, it really won't matter how exciting the vision. Followers usually will not commit to a vision unless they are committed to the leader. Thus, it's possible that a leader's influence can exceed his level of authority. Leaders are followed because of vision, and are admired for their core values and abilities. They will not be followed if they cannot be trusted.

Therefore, leaders must continually develop their skills. They must grow in knowledge and understanding and exhibit qualities that others admire. This will happen if the leader is intentional, self-motivated, and self-disciplined. A leader without self-discipline will generally fall short in the eyes of his followers.

A leader with no self-discipline
is an accident about to happen.

Leadership must be committed.

Leaders must commit to the organization. They must want the organization to succeed and be determined to work fully and completely toward that goal. Committed leaders feel personally responsible for the success of the organization. They will work tirelessly to make the business successful. Outstanding leaders who are fully committed to an organization will often put the needs of the organization above their own personal needs.

But leaders do not lead by themselves. They have followers. Good leaders build teams and relationships that allow more effective work habits and ultimately better results. People want connections. They need to feel that they are valued, trusted, and cared for. Developing good interpersonal relationships with team members helps build lasting connections that become invaluable when the work is particularly demanding.

Never forget your responsibility.

Leaders are responsible for producing the end result. If that is not done well, everything else can suffer. Every football player knows that the goal is to win the game, not just gain yardage or have good statistics. If you get too tied up in daily problems it is easy to lose focus on the goal.

Knowing the goal and purpose is just as important in business. The leaders are responsible for keeping their focus on the purpose and mission of the organization. The goal of the team must ultimately be to produce quality products or services.

PRINCIPLE #9: PLANNING

Planning, prioritizing, organizing, and executing are the most basic and fundamental responsibilities of a good leader. The success of a leader is often determined by how well he plans and prioritizes. To implement and execute effectively a leader must:

- Know what is important and attack the high priority problems first.
- Develop a plan that is clear and concise; one that everyone can understand and follow.
- Adequately analyze the situation and develop solutions with the help of team members and trusted outside sources when necessary.
- Oversee execution of the plan, ensuring that the critical focus is on high priority tasks.
- Regularly review progress and confirm that priorities have not changed.
- Communicate status up and down the line.

If there are multiple problems or multiple projects, managing for results can be stressful and sometimes overwhelming. The plan must be monitored with team members so that everyone knows what is important, where the project is going, and how well they are doing. If there are numerous critically important issues at stake, the environment can be very tense and stress is likely to impact the entire team. Priorities might change frequently resulting in a plan that changes frequently.

Good leaders will not become rattled in a high-stakes situation. They will demonstrate a calm demeanor and an attention to detail. In these situations good communication is vital for all team members. The more the entire team understands the more likely it is that the focus will remain on high priority issues and not be sidelined chasing unimportant issues. It is often easy to get overly focused on one particular issue if no one is looking at the whole picture.

It is the leader's responsibility to know the priorities and remind team members of the big picture. Team members may be shifted around to focus on the important issues. Reorganizing is the responsibility of the leader.

Good leaders never take their eyes off the purpose and mission of the organization. Leaders must continually be aware of the organization's objectives and goals. They must know the end-game and clearly communicate that to team members. If the mission or ultimate goal is not clear, the people doing the work can be confused and not understand why change is needed. Focus can be lost if workers don't know the purpose of changes because communication is lacking. The mission and purpose may need to be refined or clarified to fit with new priorities that are being communicated down the line.

Good leaders make necessary refinements or changes in plans as clear and concise as possible. In addition, when the mission changes that must be quickly and effectively communicated to team members so that the work does not lose focus, become ineffective, and prevent accomplishment of the new goals and objectives. When everyone understands the purpose and mission it is much easier to make good decisions. It is easier to implement a plan that everyone understands. Battling confusion or misunderstanding can waste both time and resources.

Planning is needed at all levels of a project. Executives make the big and broad directives and pass those down the chain of command. The planning process continues at all levels of the organization. There should be a common purpose, mission, and goal guiding the planning process.

Communication can be accomplished in one-on-one conferences, group meetings, or written communication.

Good leaders will provide ways that team members can ask questions and clarify any concerns. Good leaders will often ask leading questions of their immediate team members to ensure that they understand the issues and the new direction. If team members do not really understand what is going on, it is likely that implementation will be confused, ineffective, or slow.

The best teams and leaders will continually or frequently monitor progress. Is the plan being implemented properly and is it producing the expected results? A progress review will often ask questions such as these:

- What is working? Are the results as projected?
- What is not working? Why?
- What new issues or questions have arisen because of the changes?
- What have we learned that should trigger other changes?

PRINCIPLE #10: DELEGATION

Because leaders cannot do everything themselves, they must learn to delegate. Often delegation is necessary because someone has special and unique knowledge or capabilities that will assure a better result. Leaders consider the following in delegating responsibility:

- others are more skilled,
- another member of the team could grow and develop from the work,
- the work is recurring and should be assigned permanently, or
- more time is needed to evaluate the work of those responsible.

Experience has proven that leaders are not capable of managing dozens of people. A good leader can effectively manage six to ten subordinates, depending on his skills and capabilities. This rule of thumb assumes that the leader is truly managing on a daily basis. If subordinates are decentralized around the country and have their own significant responsibility and authority, the number of subordinates that can be effectively managed is higher.

Delegated responsibility must be accompanied by associated authority. Responsibility without authority is a losing proposition. Typically nothing happens if the authority does not exist to make it happen. Frustration will occur when subordinates without authority are held responsible for results they cannot impact.

The ability to delegate is an essential leadership quality. The more effectively this is accomplished, the more likely it is that a leader and his team will be successful. Delegation is not just assigning work, but it is giving responsibility and authority to the right person because you know he or she has the ability to do the job. The result should be that team performance and productivity is improved.

> *Good delegation gives the right work*
> *to the right person for the right reasons*
> *in order to produce the right result.*

Great leaders will empower their teams to achieve or exceed goals. Leaders must rely on good people to do good work. Otherwise the leader must do it all and that is not possible. Thus, the leader must train subordinates to take responsibility for managing the process to achieve team goals. Likewise subordinates must be prepared to use their skills and capabilities to achieve team solutions and goals.

Empowering team members to develop and use their talents will build a strong team that will be effective when their skills are needed to overcome difficulties. If the leader does not develop this capability in his team, it will be much more difficult to overcome problems. Good leaders know these skills must be developed and will have their team ready when it is necessary.

> *"As we look ahead into the next century, leaders will be those who empower others."*
> Bill Gates[20]

Good leaders will manage teams in order deliver projects completed on time and within or under budget. They want the result to be of the highest quality possible. They will manage difficulties and problems until they are overcome. They make no excuses.

Thus, delegation becomes a highly effective form of team management in order to produce excellent results.

PRINCIPLE #11: LEADERS FOLLOW

A good leader must not only lead but must follow well. Good leadership goes both up and down the chain of command. Leaders must practice what they preach and respond to superiors, just as they want their followers to communicate to them.

Leaders who do not follow well probably do not lead well. Many people with great authority are not good at leading because they are bad at following. A leader must not only lead the people on his team or group but he must manage the relationship between himself and his boss and other superiors. Thus, communications are just as important going up the chain-of-command as they are in motivating and training subordinates.

If you, as a leader, are not getting decisions or help from your superiors, make sure you are communicating clearly and concisely all appropriate information so that decisions can be made by superiors. Relationships up the chain are sometimes more important than those going to subordinates. A subordinate leader must use his experience, knowledge, and negotiation skills to communicate her ideas, needs, and requirements to her superiors. This must be done with respect, clarity, and the highest degree of professionalism possible.

Remember, bosses are juggling similar information and requests from other subordinate leaders. In essence you are competing with other good leaders as well as the budget of your superior. If you are competing with other serious projects or functions, you may need to find creative ways to convince your superior of your needs or find a new alternative solution that does not cost anything or even saves the organization money.

All teams within an organization are on the same larger team and the entire organization must be a coordinated group all moving in the same direction. It's possible that not all requests can be accommodated. One role of the subordinate leader is to support his boss and the organization. Once a decision is made, all subordinate leaders must be on board aiming at the same target. The good subordinate leader will find ways to support the decisions of the organization, while producing outstanding results by his team.

Good leaders will put aside egos and personal agendas in order to achieve the purpose and mission of the organization. Thus, the good leader manages both up and down the chain of command.

PRINCIPLE #12: MOTIVATE and INSPIRE

Followers and employees will not want to follow leaders with no emotion or passion. Good leaders are invested in their responsibilities and will demonstrate passion and emotion in inspiring others to achieve results.

Good leaders will harness the emotions of their team members to produce the very best result possible. People who suggest that emotion does not belong in the workplace don't understand the human condition. Emotions are everywhere within the work environment. Whether they are displayed will depend on the person and the work environment. Positive emotions can be very beneficial in most work situations.

Workers will often attach themselves to leaders who are "just like you and me." When followers know the names of your family, pets, and special friends, they will relate personally and the barrier between leaders and worker will be a blurred line and leaders will be more approachable.

Inspire others.

Leaders provide inspiration so that others can find meaning in a vision or purpose. Without meaning and inspiration those who follow will often have a difficult time committing themselves to the greater purpose. Inspiration helps people see that everything they do matters.

Subordinates need to know that their management has a clear vision and purpose. They want to know that the business is stable and have faith that their leaders are guiding them in the right direction. Good leaders will present a positive image, communicate hope, and encourage others to feel good about what they are doing.

Be tuned into emotions.

Don't try to eliminate emotions but manage them as necessary. Remember that a good working team will often be a very close knit unit. Emotions can arise because the work is important and the people are invested in the success of the work or project.

A good leader uses both head and heart knowledge in managing his team. It is important to be sensitive to feelings, points of view, new ideas, or anything that might create stress and anxiety if simply ignored.

CONCLUSION

Leadership principles must be carefully considered and balanced in order to ensure that the best outcome is achieved for the organization. Many of the challenges of leaders are created when they rely too heavily on one leadership principle. Excellent leadership requires that a leader be skilled in a number of areas in order to meet the needs of both employees and the organization.

The above principles describe the basic functions of the leader. All must be utilized by leaders to some degree. The better you perform on a larger number of these principles the more accomplished leader you will become.

TIPS YOU COULD USE

a. Underline, circle, or highlight the 1 to 3 principles above that you think could make the most impact if you implemented them in your life or career. You will revisit these choices at the end of the book in the Planning section.

b. There may be other things that you think would make a difference. Write them below:

_____

_____

_____

_____

_____

Wisdom to Action Challenge

Write down 3 core values that define your leadership (e.g., accountability, fairness). For the next seven days, audit one daily decision against these principles. Ask: Did my actions align with my values? How can I be a better leader in my role?

Chapter 5
Leadership Qualities

"Do not follow where the path may lead. Go instead where there is no path and leave a trail."
Ralph Waldo Emerson[22]

INTRODUCTION

In this chapter we will discuss the qualities that a good leader should possess. These are generally essential characteristics or attributes that distinguish a good leader from the average or poor leader. Good leaders will probably have all these qualities to *some* degree.

The more these qualities are present the better the leader will be. High quality leaders will utilize most of these characteristics at a high level, assuring that they have a significant degree of success in achieving team objectives and organizational goals.

Good leaders know their role and responsibilities within the organization. They will know what is expected and will manage toward the achievement of those expectations. In order for the leader to know his role, expectations need to be clearly defined and well-communicated from the organization. In turn the good leader will communicate those expectations to his team. When this does not happen confusion and frustration often result.

The following qualities are the <u>primary</u> characteristics of good leadership. They are not listed in any particular order.

Quality: KNOWING THE MISSION

One of the most important qualities is to know and understand the purpose and mission of the organization. Everything a leader says and does should be tested against the mission.

Good leaders think big, see the business in terms of its mission, and inspire others to fulfill the purpose. Thinking small, local, and always within the boundaries will not allow the organization to "go where no one has gone before." Leaders inspire and communicate their vision for the express purpose of achieving company strategic goals.

Obviously there are lower levels within an organization where this quality is not as important.

Quality: INTENTIONAL LISTENING

Followers want to be heard. Good leaders understand how important it is to listen well. When the leader listens, the team will listen. Listening goes both ways. Listening builds trust, and trust is a foundational principle of good leadership.

Leaders who fail to listen well will have a much more difficult time leading their team. Leaders must be able to hear ideas and suggestions as well as warnings of pending problems. Good leaders will ask the right questions to elicit constructive feedback. But if they are not listening well, they may miss critical information.

Followers want their leaders to listen to their ideas and be concerned about their needs. Leaders may not always accept or agree, but they do need to listen. Followers should make every attempt to ensure that their leaders understand what they are saying. But followers also want leaders to understand how they are feeling. If the leader demonstrates empathy and respect, listens well, and acknowledges the input, followers will usually be satisfied.

Leaders who listen well ensure their team members that they understand the issues and problems. If the leader allows and evaluates input from her team, they will line up behind whatever decision she ultimately makes. They will follow, not because they necessarily believe the leader made the right decision, but because their ideas were heard and considered.

Followers won't care how much you know until you demonstrate how much you care.

Active listening is a quality that can prevent problems from happening or getting out of control. Workers on the front lines will frequently see issues and problems first and can be the key to fixing problems before they become critical. They will communicate this information when they know they are being heard. If the ears of team leaders are closed, many workers will simply allow problems to occur until they become obvious to the leader.

If leaders listen with sincere attention, trusting relationships will develop that will benefit all members of the team, particularly over the long term. Active listening requires care and focus and may result in investigation into the facts and ongoing situation. This skill is sometimes the result of natural abilities, but if not, it must be developed by self-discipline and awareness.

Quality: COLLABORATION

Good leaders will work closely with their team, with other teams, with related departments, with vendors, and all other people and entities that impact the success of the team. It is often critical that good relationships be developed with outside suppliers and contractors to assure the adequate flow of goods and services. Mutual cooperation is a valuable quality for effective leaders.

Good leaders create partnerships with all those that can impact their success.

Quality: FLEXIBILITY

Rigid leaders usually don't last very long. Change is the watchword in any viable operation and leaders should be on the front lines managing change. They may even be the ones instigating change in many organizations.

The effective leader is not threatened by new ideas and concepts. Flexibility is an absolute necessity in our changing world. Change is occurring constantly and those without flexibility will be left behind, mired in out-of-date thinking and systems.

Quality: OPTIMISIM

Good leaders look on the bright side of things and have positive attitudes about life and the world in general. It is very difficult for people with negative attitudes, or those who are constantly grumbling, to inspire anyone else. Projecting optimism and positive thoughts during times of difficulties will inspire others to be positive and do better work.

Optimism frequently is accompanied by confidence, and that will give team members assurance that their management is competent and fully capable of leading through any difficulties that may arise.

Quality: PASSION

Workers are inspired toward common goals and quality commitments by passionate leaders who believe in their work. If the leader lacks passion about the work why would the workers be any different? If you are the director of a play and exhibit little passion for the performance, don't expect your actors to be any different. Followers imitate the attitudes of their leaders. If you want to lead well, you must be inspiring and passionate about what you are doing.

Effective leaders will be passionate about all aspects of the work and will expect followers to feel the same. Their passion will often be contagious to the point that all followers will have the same passion. The head janitor who is diligent and demands excellence will instill that same sense of passion in his employees and his building will shine like it was built yesterday.

Quality: PATIENCE, PERSEVERANCE, and RESILIENCE

Patience generally means the act of bearing trials calmly, not complaining, and holding fast, even in the presence of opposition. Patient people do not make hasty decisions. Patient people are also persistent. They will persevere under whatever circumstances exist because they know that time is sometimes required to achieve goals.

Good leaders will not be deterred and if time is necessary to achieve interim objectives, they will be reasonably patient with mistakes, misunderstandings, and delays caused by others outside their control. But, although they may be patient, their focus will not waver from priorities and commitments.

Leaders demand excellence, but realize that excellence and patience can be difficult to balance. Good leaders never take their eyes off the goal. They have their focus on the big picture, knowing that it is the ultimate mission that must be achieved. Current difficulties are simply battles that must be won in order to win the war.

Good leaders don't give up. They are in the game for the long term and know that achieving desired results does not always occur immediately. The situation may require new systems, new skills, new technology, and even new people. They will not allow setbacks to deter them from achieving their goals.

Resilient leaders will not be stopped by operational problems that must be resolved and overcome. They will maintain their focus and energy until the desired result is achieved.

You must understand yourself before taking responsibility for others. Resilient leaders are perceptive and also know how to handle themselves in any good or bad situations.

Resilience is similar to perseverance but is usually meant to imply the ability to recover from misfortune. It is certainly safe to conclude that being patient, resilient, and able to persevere are excellent leadership qualities.

Resilient leaders are high performing
individuals who overcome diversity
with positive energy.

Quality: SELF-AWARENESS

Self-aware leaders know their own strengths and weaknesses as well as those of their team. They do not put themselves or their team in a position to fail because necessary knowledge, skills, or capabilities are not present.

Good leaders will recognize their own shortcomings as well as those of their team and take actions to correct weaknesses. They will also bring in outside experts when special skills are required. They will not expect people to perform at levels outside their capabilities. Good leaders ask for help when needed. Being honest and transparent about capabilities can prevent embarrassing failures that can leave scars on both the leader and the team.

Leaders who are self-aware know the boundaries and limits of themselves as well as their team. Good leaders will delegate work for which they do not have particular strengths. They will give such responsibility to more gifted, skilled, or more knowledgeable members of the team.

Good leaders will not put subordinates in a position to fail. It is one thing to give a subordinate work that will challenge him and allow him to grow. It is another thing to give someone responsibility that is beyond his capabilities. Good leaders will work together with subordinates in order to train and educate them in the necessary skills to complete difficult tasks.

Quality: TRANSPARENCY AND OPENNESS

Having an open environment and frequent communication will help teams accomplish the work and grow at the same time. Good leaders will encourage questions and have open discussions about ways to solve problems or overcome deficiencies. Employees who have certain skills can be partnered with employees who are still learning the necessary skills in order to achieve better results.

Teaching someone else is a good skill to develop in more talented employees. It allows employees to respect others who are still learning because they are given the responsibility of training them. Teaching and training others is also a good first step in growing new leaders.

Good leaders openly communicate with their team. Secrets between management and employees generally lead to mistrust and suspicion. Keeping employees up-to-date with progress, both good and bad, allows the team to focus on the work and not be concerned about what information is not being shared.

Leaders who are open, real, and sincere will have followers who are the same. Confidence breeds confidence and open communication and transparency will duplicate itself in employees if it is demonstrated by leaders.

Leaders must live and operate in a state of reality. You cannot talk and act as though things are perfect when they are not. True leaders acknowledge the truth and deal with problems in an open and transparent environment. They don't try to cover up problems or weaknesses, because that will just make things worse.

Good leaders investigate and confirm problems and then set about fixing them in whatever manner is required.

Great leaders identify and fix problems!

Quality: SELF-CONFIDENCE

Leaders must have confidence in themselves. Leaders with little self-confidence will have few followers. Subordinates will be reluctant to follow leaders who don't believe in themselves or their own capabilities. Good leaders will have a solid self-image and will be confident that if a problem develops they can accurately analyze it and fix it.

Self-confidence is critical for leading others. Confidence combined with passion can be important motivators for accomplishing team goals. Leaders who are confident are able to be decisive when decisions are required.

> *"You have to have confidence in your ability and be tough enough to follow through."*
> Rosalynn Carter[24]

If you don't have confidence in your decisions or yourself, nobody else will either. Leaders must exhibit confidence even when they have questions in their own minds. How would you feel if your team leader made an important decision and then said he was not really confident this was going to work and hoped nobody would lose their jobs if the undertaking failed?

If I were a team member, I would be getting my resume up-to-date.

In order to inspire followers or team members, a good leader will exude confidence in his and the organization's decisions. Uncertainty by the people required to carry out a decision can be a self-fulfilling prophecy. If you expect something to fail, it often will. If questions surround the undertaking, people will not want to put their name on something they think is suspect.

Good leaders will convince team members and anyone responsible for executing a decision that their best efforts are required. Leaders must inspire confidence and display certainty in their decisions. That attitude must be relayed to others along with an understanding of the bigger picture in order to assure subordinates they are on a track to success.

A good leader supports the mission of the organization. That attitude will be relayed down the chain of command and instill belief in what is to be accomplished. Troubles are created when the purpose, mission, or plan are not explicitly clear. Workers can see through half-hearted support and if it is not addressed, such doubt can ambush a project before it even gets started.

Communications are critically important in the midst of important decisions because innocent misunderstanding can create doubt and fear. If lower level leaders, without adequate knowledge, believe that decisions are not aligned with the organization's stated goals or values, confidence must be restored. All levels of management must feel comfortable asking questions up the chain-of-command if they have serious doubts.

If a leader or group of leaders cannot understand or see the wisdom of some decision, they need to examine it thoroughly until they can become confident in its purpose. If they still cannot buy into the decision, they must take their concern up the organization until they do feel confident. Once they understand, they can then implement the decision and move forward in confidence. Thus, executive members of an organization need to be prepared to inspire their frontline leadership teams in the purpose and strategy behind major decisions.

The "what" to be done is certainly necessary for critical decisions, but so is the "why." If the people implementing change do not know the "why," they will generally have little confidence in the "what" they are doing. Leaders at _all_ levels must understand the purposes behind decisions so they can wholeheartedly support them.

> *"Leaders must be tough enough to fight, tender enough to cry, human enough to make mistakes, humble enough to admit them, strong enough to absorb the pain, and resilient enough to bounce back and keep on moving."*
> Jesse Jackson[25]

Quality: VISION

Leaders with vision can understand the future and perceive the needs and desires in that future environment. Not every good leader is a visionary, but those organizations that have such a leader should utilize that skill or gift to advance their business. Visionary leaders will spend significant amounts of time trying to understand new developments. They keep themselves updated on important visionary thinking.

But all leaders need some visionary abilities. They need to be able to project the end result. They must understand the nature of the organization's purpose and mission and what that means and implies in their work environment. This visionary ability will allow leaders to experiment and take reasonable risks within their sphere of influence.

> *"The very essence of leadership is that you have vision. You can't blow an uncertain trumpet."*
> Theodore M. Hesburgh[26]

Quality: SELF-MOTIVATION

Leaders who cannot motivate themselves will find it difficult to motivate or inspire others. Motivating team members is a function of the team leader. It may even be a required quality. But it starts with the leader.

Therefore the good leader will be passionate and excited about the work to be accomplished and will be able to motivate others to share that same passion.

> *"The great leaders of business, industry, and finance, and the great artists, poets, musicians and writers all became great because they developed the power of self-motivation."*
> Napoleon Hill[27]

Quality: SELF-DISCIPLINE

Effective leaders have good or excellent self-discipline and develop that quality in their subordinates. Self-disciplined people require much less oversight. Once they understand what is required or necessary they can manage their own time and effort to accomplish a task. Self-disciplined leaders and workers are highly respected and can set the example for a good work ethic for other workers.

This is a necessary quality in a workplace that can often be very hectic. People with self-discipline can be trusted to organize their schedule and work effort to accomplish the goals of the team and organization. For additional information on self-discipline see Appendix A.

> *"Great leaders always have self-discipline – without exception."*
> John C. Maxwell[28]

Quality: EMOTIONAL STRENGTH

Emotions and feelings must be managed carefully in order that they not disrupt the work or cause decisions to be made on the basis of feelings that do not represent reality. Leaders must manage their own emotions as well as deal with the feelings and emotions of subordinates.

Managing emotions and feelings means that a leader is aware of emotional influences and is able to distinguish between feelings that have meaning in the workplace and those that do not. Feelings and emotions are neither good nor bad; they just "are." They exist, and good leaders must identify, evaluate, and understand their importance.
In general, feelings and emotions should not influence work decisions. Good leaders will have empathy for the existence of feelings, but will make decisions based on the facts of the situation at hand. Good leaders will take control of situations where emotions are involved and guide the team to decisions that are consistent with the facts and the organization. Good leaders will also have social and interpersonal skills that can be used to resolve emotional issues and arrive at wise business decisions.

Quality: SUPPORT SYSTEMS

The saying that "No one person can do it all" gives us great insight in thinking about a support system. In this case it is not necessarily others who can help do the actual work, but a network of friends and advisors who can provide advice, encouragement, or ideas. They can be great sounding boards.

Many good leaders acquired leadership skills because they had a mentor who provided wise support and advice when training and education was needed. A support network is not in the trenches with you but will provide help in navigating the problems you discover in those trenches. Mentors and advisors can be invaluable when new or particularly difficult situations arise.

Having a network of people that you can go to for advice is an extremely valuable resource. Often the reality about a situation is not obvious to the one involved. The situation can often be seen more realistically by someone who is not under the immediate pressure of the moment. When issues or problems are particularly difficult, trusted mentors can be invaluable.

Good leaders will in turn be mentors and trainers for their team. Leaders will build trust by providing encouragement, instruction, advice, and commitment. They support teamwork and encourage their people to help others when appropriate.

> *"Leadership without support is like trying to make bricks without enough straw. True leaders reinforce their ideas and plans with strategic partnerships, alliances, and supportive audiences."*
> Reed Markham[29]

Quality: LEARN QUICKLY

Good leaders will adapt to new ways, understand quickly the nature of the business, and develop understanding and wisdom in dealing with subordinates, bosses, vendors, and customers. People who are slow learners or slow to adapt will soon be left behind.

Often decisions must be made quickly in order to resolve serious problems. Taking time to test out many possible alternatives may not be possible. Processes and systems that worked well in the past can quickly become outdated and obsolete in today's world.

The crisis of COVID changed the landscape almost overnight. New plans and strategies for the work environment had to be implemented in a very short time. Leaders must be able to evaluate and analyze new trends and develop new strategies and systems to stay competitive. During COVID there was no time to try different solutions until a desirable solution could be found. Many of those who utilized this strategy failed or are still trying to recover.

Future events can create uncertainties when everything seems to be running smoothly. Those organizations that survived COVID were able to act quickly and with intelligent insight to survive or thrive in the crisis.

Good leaders have a bias toward taking action. They will fail on the side of doing something rather than on playing it safe. They don't take unreasonable risks but neither do they take forever to make decisions. Leaders are prepared to move quickly and have good reason for doing so. Changing just to act quickly can be a fool's graveyard. Don't be afraid to err if the reward is worth it but don't implement change just because it is exciting and might energize the team.

Damian McKinney, the CEO of McKinney Rogers and author of *The Commando Way* has said, "The ability to take decisive actions in the face of uncertainty and dynamic environments are critical capabilities for an organization." But you can only do this with good leaders!

When all employees have a clear vision of the mission, know the products, and are empowered to act, even dynamic changes in the marketplace can be overcome by effective and timely responses.

TIPS YOU COULD USE

a. Underline, circle, or highlight the 1 to 3 qualities above that you think could make the most impact if you implemented them in your life or career. You will revisit these choices at the end of the book in the Planning section.

b. There may be other things that you think would make a difference. Write them below:

_____

_____

_____

_____

THE DICHOTOMY OF LEADERSHIP QUALITIES

The function of being a leader has some interesting relationships that can seem contradictory or at least confusing at first glance. A leader may be doing something on one front but seem to be doing something else at cross purposes at the same time. For example, someone in leadership is both a follower and a leader.

Principle #11 in the previous chapter is an obvious dichotomy. A leader must follow his superiors and lead his subordinates. He does both, and he needs to do both well. Following are additional examples of the dichotomies of leadership.

A leader must be both calm and passionate.

Emotions and feelings should _not_ be the basis for decisions. A good leader should be passionate about her work and her team but feelings and emotions cannot drive decisions. Feelings and emotions can impact the quality of decisions to the detriment of the team or the organization. However, leaders should not be emotionless robots. Good leaders will have passion for their work and empathy for team members.

A leader must be confident.

Confidence can be contagious within a team atmosphere. Thus, it is important that such confidence be based on sound reasoning and analysis. It should not be the kind of confidence that appears to be arrogance or the result of emotions that are not under control.

> *People do not follow robots*
> *or pride-filled leaders.*

A leader must be cautious as well as brave.

Being brave or having courage does not mean that one undertakes unnecessary risk or engages in foolish actions.

The enemy of the confident and courageous leader is that he becomes overconfident and reckless. The urge to take on any challenge must be controlled. The overall goal is to achieve the mission. That mission can be damaged if it is subordinate to a leader's foolish bravado.

Reputations can be destroyed because a leader did not understand or account for the dangers and risks of his actions. Evaluating the risk of taking certain actions is an important responsibility of the leader. In some situations it may be appropriate to take big risks, but in others the best course of action may be to take very little risk.

A Leader must be both competitive and gracious.

Good leaders will push their teams and organizations to follow their ideas and plans. When these plans are successful, all should be commended and receive the appropriate credit for work well done. When such plans fail the good leader takes the responsibility for his team and shoulders the loss. In some cases it may be necessary to be gracious to other teams who were more successful.

A competitive spirit must not drive a leader to make decisions or advance ideas that are not in the best interest of the organization. Personal recognition cannot be a driving force in making decisions.

A leader must know the details but not micromanage.

A good leader does not over manage his subordinates. It is important that leaders understand the work but not try to do it. Leaders must be focused on the bigger picture and understand the mission, but in order to do that they also must understand the work that team members are performing. A leader who gets pulled into the minutia of the work may lose perspective and focus.

A leader must produce results now but manage the team to succeed in the long run.

A good leader must be patient and focus on the long term, but current results are also frequently mandatory. The team must be managed to perform at a high current level, yet maintain an acceptable level of performance over the long haul. It is very much like running a marathon. If you treat the work as a sprint, the team may never be able to finish the race.

A company should be managed to produce a high current result, but not to the detriment of continuing to work at a high performance level for the long term. Leaders must recognize limitations and know how to pace themselves and their teams so that they can maintain a solid ongoing performance indefinitely.

A leader must be humble, listen well, but not be silent.

Leaders must think of the needs of others and even put them first at times. They must not always put their own needs at the top of the priority list. They must listen to the concerns of subordinates. But it is the leader who has the responsibility and in the end it is his job to make decisions that conform to the needs of the organization.

A leader must speak when it matters. Leaders represent both the positions of their team and the goals of the organization. If decisions are made that will negatively impact the organization, they must speak up.

A leader must know his employees but not be too close.

A good leader understands the nature of the boss and subordinate relationship. He should know his team members well and have knowledge of their personal lives and motivations. But the good leader will be cautious in engaging in the personal lives of subordinates. When leaders grow very close to team members, it can become very difficult to be the boss. Other team members may assume that such friendly relationships are impacting their own standing within the team.

Wisdom to Action Challenge

Identify one skill you've neglected (e.g., active listening, conflict resolution). Dedicate 15 minutes daily to practicing it—whether through role-playing, reading, or real-world application. Journal: How did this intentional growth impact your confidence or ability to inspire others?

Chapter 6
Ethical Leadership Characteristics
(High Personal Character)

"Success is more permanent when you achieve it without destroying your principles."
Walter Cronkite[47]

Ethical leadership is the ability to lead people and make the right decisions based on a pre-defined set of core values such as honesty, integrity, equality, and respect. Ethical practices and high personal character are often the way outstanding leaders distinguish themselves. They stand firm on a set of core values that they will not violate under any condition.

These values are based on an understanding of what is right and what is wrong. They are based on either personal core values or the organization's moral principles. Right or wrong is not determined based on the circumstances of a situation but on a set of standards that will not vary depending on circumstances because they represent the absolute core values for the organization.

The following characteristics are not listed in any particular order, other than #1, "Honesty." It is not necessarily meaningful to say that one ethical characteristic is more important than another because that implies they could be modified or changed to fit the situation. But in our opinion honesty, integrity, and truth must come before all else.

Truth is the absolute foundational core value. If it is not treated as such, life and business generally will not go well.

Honesty is very much like communication. It is inherent in most all the other personal characteristics. You cannot be trustworthy and be dishonest. Honesty and integrity must be the foundation for accountability, equality, fairness, respect, etc.

All of these ethical characteristics fit together to make the whole, but honesty and truth are the glue that holds them together. They are melded together to produce a foundation for leading, making good decisions, producing excellent work, and achieving organizational objectives. They are not mutually exclusive.

Ethics: HONESTY, INTEGRITY, and TRUTH

Leaders must know the truth, speak the truth, and reward the truth. There is nothing more basic for leaders to understand. The absolute rule is "Be truthful." Lies about people, products, and capabilities have destroyed many a good leader and many organizations.

Live your life and operate
your career based on truth!

Integrity and honesty are core values that all leaders <u>must</u> possess. A business of any size will not compete or survive unless employees are honest, practice integrity, and live their personal and business lives based on truth. Leaders who do not display these qualities cannot be trusted to lead an organization. Ultimately they will fail and probably do great damage to the organization.

Personal character is an integral part of the makeup of excellent leaders. If leaders cannot be trusted, are dishonest, and take no responsibility for their actions, the organization has little hope for success, even if such leaders have many other good leadership qualities. Therefore, the personal and ethical character of leadership is an important and integral requirement for success.

Honesty, integrity, and truth must start at the top and run all through an organization. Subordinates at any level will imitate the core values of senior leaders. Senior leaders must emphasize and demonstrate these qualities and encourage them throughout their organization.

No matter the circumstances, core values of an organization are not to be violated. In well-run organizations, anyone found violating the core values of the organization will be fired immediately. Good leaders demand that all core values be adhered to.

Anything that is morally corrupt or illegal should be rejected out of hand. Employees should be encouraged to report any such occurrences to management.

> *"Leadership can be defined by one word: 'honesty'. You must be honest with the players and honest with yourself."*
> Earl Weaver[30]

It is really not that difficult to know what is right. You inherently follow or obey an internal code of conduct. Most people know what is right. The only issue is whether or not you will act according to what you know is right. There is often financial gain and power at stake and those can be powerful influences on your core values. Peer pressure and direct instructions from superiors can also challenge your personal core values.

Ethical leadership comes down to each individual deciding if he or she is willing to violate their core values, regardless of whether or not a Code of Conduct exists. Good leaders build their careers on a set of core values regardless of whether their organization has a Code of Conduct. Those values vary between individuals but will normally include most of the characteristics discussed in this chapter.

In general, honesty, respect, and trust are the centerpieces of a Code of Conduct. Valued leaders are always accountable for their words and actions. If a good leader makes a mistake he should be the first to openly admit it. The focus becomes on correctly identifying the error and finding effective solutions, not on blame, shame, or censure. A leader who wants honesty and integrity from his team must exhibit those same characteristics himself.

A good leader's values include equal opportunity. Equal opportunity does not mean that bad work and poor performance is tolerated. An outstanding leader demands excellence from all followers. Everyone should be educated and trained to perform at high levels. Those who cannot perform must be moved down or back in the organization until they can perform at the desired levels.

Ethics: TRUST

Good leaders will delegate responsibilities to their trusted junior leaders. A leader will trust her team to carry out normal and special projects. Delegation demonstrates trust in subordinates and that trust will normally go both up and down the chain of command.

Great teams are built on trust and cooperation. If you cannot completely trust your partner, your team members, your family, or your co-workers, everything will probably fall apart. Trust is the cement that holds relationships together. When trust is lost, high performance teams, no matter how skilled, will lose their edge and probably fail.

Good leaders are candid about the capabilities of subordinates.

Trust is one of the very important qualities of a leader because a leader must be trusted by the team to make the right decisions. If subordinates do not trust the decisions of the leader it will be difficult for the leader to marshal the cooperation and commitment to tackle the job. Trust is linked very closely with employee commitment and engagement to achieve goals.

Honesty and truth are generally considered the number one requirements for garnering trust in any group situation. A lack of honesty will not only reflect poorly on the leader but will also reflect back on the organization. If the leader or management personnel are not trustworthy, then it is unlikely that the organization is any better.

There are seven other practices that will help build trust:

1. Work together

Good leaders will interact with and often participate in the daily activities of the team. Employees benefit greatly by interacting closely with leaders. Demonstrating that you want your subordinates to grow and develop in their careers will open lines of communication and also indicate you value their input and opinions.

2. Give others credit

Always recognize the accomplishments of the team and team members. Give credit to the team when there are successes and take responsibility for mistakes and problems. Never publically call out the team for criticism. Discuss problems and issues in private. Demonstrate an attitude of putting the team first and yourself second. Make every effort to praise work that is well done.

3. Demonstrate mutual respect

If you want to receive loyalty and trust you must provide respect and trust. Mutual respect is a foundation for trust. A caring leader will demonstrate that a person is as important as the work. Sharing and openness without negative talk and complaining will create an environment of trust. Gossip, grumbling, dishonesty, or insincerity will not create a foundation of mutual respect.

4. Connect personally

Good leaders will connect with team members in order to create emotional and intellectual connections or bonds. It is much easier to interact when there is a personal connection because you understand the impact of emotions, feelings, and moods that others are experiencing that may impact their job performance. You should know your employees personally, but not necessarily intimately.

5. Admit mistakes

As a leader, you become real to your subordinates when you admit errors, mistakes, or poor judgment. Failure is not necessarily a good thing, but it can be used to gain understanding and build better working relationships. Sincerity and truth require that you not only admit mistakes but demonstrate how to deal with setbacks on a positive basis.

Everyone makes mistakes and good leaders do not want employees hiding them. The best way to avoid hiding mistakes is to demonstrate that the focus around mistakes is finding solutions, not casting blame.

6. Maintain high personal values

People trust others who stay true to their personal core values and the standards of the organization. Maintaining core values will create respect and trust in a team or organization. When everyone shares similar values it is much easier to make the right decisions and stand on ethical principles, regardless of the result. Business may be lost and projects might be late, but core values are not violated.

7. Servant leadership

Servant leadership is often at the core of building a trust relationship with employees. Putting the team first will create two-way communication that helps establish a mindset of respect and trust. Successful leaders give without necessarily expecting anything in return, other than cooperation, diligence, and a helpful attitude.

Trust must exist up and down the chain of command. The blame game can destroy an organization. Leaders and workers should be unified by a common goal. Hidden agendas can and will destroy the ability to be successful. Transparency and honest communication are trademarks of an atmosphere where trust is paramount. Again, honesty is foundational in establishing trust.

Open conversations and honest feedback also facilitate trusting relationships. The result of trust is an environment where support and encouragement are present. People are not fearful of taking responsibility for their work. Safe communication is possible and everyone is working toward the same goal. Thoughts, feelings, beliefs, and ideas can be shared openly in this kind of environment.

Leaders with character rely on trust and respect to gain cooperation.

Ethics: ACCOUNTABILITY

Accountability means that the leader accepts responsibility for his actions and those of his team. It may mean taking responsibility for falling short of goals, fulfilling promises, and being held accountable for the mistakes of others. Taking responsibility for poor decisions or mistakes demonstrates an ability to stand up for others. Subordinates make mistakes, but that does not mean that a leader will sacrifice a team member.

In today's world everyone wants to find someone to blame. I can tell you that people of high character do not make casting blame and finding scapegoats a matter of interest. For example if you listen to the interviews on Sunday afternoon following an NFL football game, you will almost always find the losing quarterback taking the blame for a loss.

While every employee is accountable, it is particularly critical for leaders. A leader's lack of accountability can negatively influence the entire team and seriously impact results. Just as team members are held accountable, so must the leader take responsibility for his performance.

A culture of accountability allows everyone on the team to understand what is expected. It also allows leaders to expect excellence. Team members can become more effective and creative when they understand what is expected and are given the tools to succeed.

"Accountability is the glue that ties commitment to the result."
Bob Practor[32]

Ethics: EQUALITY

Effective leaders do not ignore or shy away from diversity. They use it to enhance the strengths of their team. People of different personalities, backgrounds, and cultures will bring the possibility of new and better solutions when combined with existing methods. Diversity can also be the catalyst for innovative ways for doing things that lead to growth and higher profits.

Unfortunately the human condition seems to love to discriminate against others. The reasons for this discrimination vary, and most are complete nonsense. Typically the problem centers around race or gender but they can extend to hair color, speech patterns, clothing, and anything else that someone wants to use to feel superior over another.

The world is diverse! Good leaders hire good people regardless of color, creed, gender, or lifestyle. Today's world is very competitive and the intent of every good leader should be to hire the very best people possible. Diversity is often a key to a successful work environment because it brings together different ideas and customs that can produce the best end result.

Good leaders are not slow to bring diversity to the workplace. They will also provide a safe and comfortable workplace where everyone has the opportunity to grow and advance. Training for employees should be available to allow all employees to advance.

All types of discrimination are abhorrent and have absolutely no value in the workplace. If you practice discrimination you risk being in conflict with moral, local, and national laws. If you want to be a leader, you must be prepared to deal with the diversity of a global workplace.

Ethics: HUMILITY

Leaders who are humble servant leaders stand out as the most effective in getting cooperation and production from followers. People gravitate to leaders who they know have their best interests at heart. Humble individuals who give thought to the needs and desires of others are very attractive leaders.

Humble leaders will often put the needs of others above their own. They will respect the ideas and feedback of subordinates. They will allow others to make decisions in accordance with their capabilities.

Humility is not necessarily among the traits often considered when people talk about leadership qualities. Humility is a very personal characteristic. It is generally not considered in the same category with the more dynamic and practical qualities that reflect personality and other skills that are "commanding" in nature.

Humble leaders know that people want honesty and transparency backed up by wisdom and understanding that will produces results. Followers know all the tricks of prideful leaders who have only their own interests at heart. They will quickly gravitate to humble men and women who put employees' needs and wants at a level at least equal with their own.

Humility can go a long way in establishing mutual respect, sincerity, confidence, and trust. Humility recognizes that all team members, including the leader, can learn and grow in their responsibilities. Humble leaders recognize that there is always more to learn and that they do not necessarily have all the answers. These attitudes will earn respect and loyalty from subordinates.

Ethics: EMPATHY

Good leaders are aware of the feelings and concerns of others. Morale can suffer if employees are hurting, grieving, sick, or depressed. These conditions can exist at any time and good leaders will be conscious of what is happening with team members. Thus, communications may need to be delivered in different formats when people are being impacted by difficult circumstances in their lives.

Empathy is more than being sympathetic or kind-hearted. It's the ability to understand and share the feelings of another. In a business environment it is particularly important to try to understand and see issues from the point of view of the subordinate. Thus, employee issues and questions are not rejected without consideration and good reason. The good leader will make every attempt to understand the point of view of subordinates, even when it is obvious he will not be able to conform to their perspective.

Leaders who are truly empathetic will be able to respond in ways that demonstrate they understand the issues. They may not be able to respond positively, but there will be a mutual understanding of the issues.

Having empathy for team members does not mean that a leader changes a business decision. It means that the message may be delivered in a different environment or in a different way to ensure that it is clearly understood. Praise and correction must be delivered to struggling workers but it must be done in ways that are constructive.

Good leaders understand the needs of others and what might be impacting their job performance. They are perceptive, aware of workers' feelings, and know how team members are thinking and feeling. This does not mean the leader can fix or even that they should attempt to fix the worker's personal issues, but understanding the situation allows leaders to communicate more effectively and modify their expectations when necessary.

Being compassionate or empathetic means a leader is conscious of his subordinates' circumstances, business and personal, and will make decisions to help that subordinate succeed. For example, if a subordinate has lost a close family member to death, that employee may be hurting for a significant period of time. A compassionate leader will allow a reasonable time for that employee to recover and return to acceptable levels of performance.

A good leader will know her team members well enough that she will not put them in situations where it would be difficult or impossible for them to succeed.

> *"Leadership is about empathy. It is about having the ability to relate to and connect with people for the purpose of inspiring and empowering their lives."*
> Oprah Winfrey[33]

Ethics: RESPECT

Good leaders exhibit respect to both followers and superiors. They treat others how they would want to be treated.

Respect means that you exhibit regard for the needs and wishes of others. You extend some form of deference to their needs, position, or their abilities. Respect does not mean that you always agree with their feelings. You do, however recognize that they have the right to hold certain beliefs just as you can hold beliefs that are different or even opposed.

Today we live in an environment where people are not the same and do not have the same values or beliefs. You must respect those differences unless they cause rebellion, refusal to do the work, create violence, or try to force their beliefs on you or others.

Respect does not necessarily mean that you like or admire someone. We all have some qualities that warrant admiration and others not so much. As a leader of a team you are primarily concerned about the quality and quantity of the work, not that you agree with anyone's personal beliefs or causes.

Ethics: FAIRNESS

Good leaders exhibit fairness when dealing with employees and others in their sphere of influence. That does not mean they will favor a subordinate over making the best decision for the organization. Unfairness, whether true or perceived, can destroy the morale of a team, but the values of the organization generally trump the values of the team members.

Good leaders communicate information to team members when it may appear that an unfair or biased decision has been implemented. All members may not agree but they will recognize that the leader was interested in openly communicating about the situation and willing to listen to their input. This openness will go a long way in establishing trust in the organization.

Since fairness is often central to the way employees expect to be treated, they will in turn treat others fairly. Treating some people better than others will cause jealousy and produce claims of favoritism. Workers have rebelled, quit, and even caused harm to other workers when they perceived they were not treated fairly.

This means that discipline or correction must be administered fairly as well. A leader cannot fire one employee for dishonesty (for example, stealing company supplies) and only warn another. They must be treated alike. But this does not mean that employees should always be treated the same. Good employees should be rewarded more than poor employees. Extremely inept or disruptive employees must be let go.

TIPS YOU COULD USE

a. Underline, circle, or highlight the 1 to 3 ethical

characteristics above that you think could make the most impact if you implemented them in your life or career. You will revisit these choices at the end of the book in the Planning section.

b. There may be other things that you think would make a difference. Write them below:

_____

_____

_____

CODE OF CONDUCT FOR ORGANIZATION

Most large companies publish a document called a Code of Conduct or a list of Core Values. They may be referred to as Standards of Business Conduct (SBC). Some firms provide training and education to all their employees on these company values. These may include rules for certain relationships between other employees, vendors, or customers. Of course, putting these values and rules on paper does not ensure that the rules will be followed.

Often an organization's Code is only as good as the character of its senior management. If the leaders of a company do not follow the Code, don't expect the employees to be any different. But the reality is that the decision to stand for honesty and character is a personal decision and following a Code of Conduct should not be dependent on how others choose to act.

If you follow the news today, unfortunately you will read story after story where leadership or employees failed to operate under a Code of Conduct, whether it was formally established by the organization or not.

The UK Institute of Business Ethics report that:

- 63% of managers have been asked to do something contrary to their own ethical values,
- 43% have been told to behave in direct violation of their organization's own Code of values, and
- 9% have been asked to break the law.[34]

In addition to personal character requirements, a Code of Conduct will often include such subjects as:

- Loyalty and unconditional support for the organization's purpose or mission.
- Encouragement and support for fellow employees.
- Treating co-workers, customers, and vendors with respect.
- Openness, trust, and reliance on each other within the organization.
- Favoritism and politics.

"The ultimate measure of a man is not where he stands in moments of comfort and convenience, but where he stands at times of challenge and controversy."
Martin Luther King, Jr.[35]

Wisdom to Action Challenge

Recall a recent ethical dilemma. Revisit it through the lens of integrity: What would you do differently if prioritizing honesty over convenience? Share your reflections with a trusted peer to reinforce accountability.

Chapter 7
Twelve Leadership Techniques

"If your actions inspire others to dream more, earn more, do more and become more, you are a leader."
John Quincy Adams[36]

In the previous chapters we described the characteristics and qualities of a good leader. If you were preparing a job description for a position that required leadership you would include many of those qualities as job requirements.

Leadership techniques are similar but they focus more specifically on special skills or concepts that a good leader might use to do a better job. Utilizing these techniques will assist the leader in distinguishing herself above other leaders or making it easier to achieve results.

Good leaders use these techniques, practices, or concepts to improve their leadership capabilities in order to achieve organization objectives. They are used to improve their effectiveness in directing the activities of subordinates. Good leaders will always be looking for ways to be more effective in leading their teams. The following techniques are proven and established concepts that can help leaders improve their performance.

1. USE WISDOM AND UNDERSTANDING

Good leadership occurs because of wisdom and understanding, not because of knowledge. Everyone knows that water exists and will flow downhill. However, understanding and wisdom will harness a river and create energy. There is a big difference between knowledge and understanding, because understanding goes beyond the basic facts, making it more useful, valuable, productive, or serviceable.

Our present society has too much data and information and too few leaders who can harness that information through understanding. Good leaders seek wisdom in order to produce better results.

2. ENCOURAGE INNOVATION

Innovation is a skill often used in managing change. Managing change is the overall principle, and innovation is a technique. Good leaders are inquisitive and not afraid to investigate and try new things. They encourage creativity and brainstorming in their teams. Good leaders want their employees thinking outside the box – how some unrelated system or technology could be applied to their work process and improve the outcome.

An innovative leader is not necessarily creative himself, but he seeks out ideas from subordinates or the marketplace that could change and even revolutionize present systems. The biggest detriment to change in the workplace is a leader who is afraid to innovate. There are often new and effective ways to build a better widget, but no leaders or organizations willing to risk change. Innovative leaders are open and willing to investigate and try new ideas.

Innovative leaders are frequently involved in outside interests where they are exposed to new and different ways of doing things. They are often voracious readers and pursue different interests. They frequently are people who have broad interests in music, art, technology, and science. Curious people recognize innovation because they are constantly being exposed to different concepts and ideas.

Leaders and teams that have the freedom to operate within reasonable boundaries will tend to be more creative. This type of freedom will give team members confidence that their leadership is not obsolete. Leaders who are open to curiosity, creativity, and innovation help their team members catch the vision or mission of the organization. Long term success is more likely with innovative leadership.

Innovation often goes hand-in-hand with simplification. Making things simple is often a time and resource saver. It is also easier to examine and evaluate new ideas if concepts and operations are simple.

Innovative leaders are not quick to reject new ideas. Instead, they will be excited about them and will encourage their team members to suggest new and sometimes even crazy ideas or solutions to problems. Unfortunately, some leaders dismiss any idea that originates with someone else.

It takes real skill and extraordinary ability to think up and refine new ways and new concepts. It takes much less effort to refine or modify someone else's good idea. Many outstanding organizations have been built on the ideas of others because someone was able to understand the possibilities or was much better at implementation.

"Innovations distinguish between
a leader and a follower."
Steve Jobs[37]

3. DEMAND EXCELLENCE

Leaders who want the best results will require the best from their followers. Good leaders set high standards and require conformance to those standards. The leader who accepts mediocrity will get mediocrity. Standards should not be unreasonable, but people who accept low standards will never get excellence. On the other hand, those who expect and demand excellence will get it.

The very best leaders require excellence from their subordinates. Excellence cannot be attained unless it is established as the expectation for every employee. Good leaders are the foundation for obtaining outstanding performance results. They will get the best out of their subordinates, often simply because they require it.

A leader who demands little will get little. It is not a disaster if subordinates feel out of their comfort zone. It is often only in that discomfort zone that the mettle of high performing people can be identified and exhibited. But the leader must also get in that zone with his team members. Good leaders hold themselves to the same or higher standards as their subordinates.

You get what you demand – so demand excellence!

4. KEEP IT SIMPLE

Simplification is often the key to success. When things are complicated only the most talented individuals can make sense of a problem. This put tremendous pressure on a limited number of people. Stress and anxiety will often cause problems to spiral out of control because they are too difficult for the team members to deal with. The result can cause chaos in the team until the problem is resolved.

One of the biggest dangers in today's workplace is making operations so complicated that no one really understands the systems and processes. Good leaders simplify whenever possible. They communicate clearly and concisely. Innovation that simplifies is rewarded and creativity is an attribute that is highly valued.

If the work or process is difficult to understand, team members will not understand their jobs or how they fit into the bigger picture. No matter how accurately instructions are communicated, if they are not understood, failure is the most likely result. Thus, in situations that border on being complicated it is critical to provide an avenue where team members can ask questions, suggest alternatives, and clarify instructions.

Good leaders are never stuck in the old rut of "We have always done it that way." Better procedures are encouraged in an effort to simplify and operate more efficiently. Good leaders will take reasonable risks to find better ways to accomplish existing tasks. Simplification makes life easier.

5. AVOID EGOTISM

The term "ego" can be described as one's sense of identity. It's the part of our personality that we think of and experience as "self." Some definitions expand ego to include the opinion we have of ourselves. In its purest sense, ego is not a negative. It's our sense of self-esteem. However, when a person is overly absorbed in himself, self-centered, or has an exaggerated sense of self-importance, we say he is "egotistical." Then, egotism becomes a negative, and this is the characteristic we will discuss in this section.

Egotism will cause disruption, anxiety, criticism, cloudy communication, and just general unease. It is a form of self-preservation. Good leaders cannot afford to let their ego get in the way of progress or success.

Egotism can prevent learning from mistakes. Constructive criticism is generally taboo where egotism reigns. Egotism can prevent any real creative discovery. If the problem exists in a leader, the work environment can be an uneasy place. It is difficult, if not impossible, to deal with, communicate with, and work with people who have inflated egos.

Egotism can allow truth to be shaded in ways that prevent seeing reality. Personal desires and protection can take precedence over organizational priorities and goals.

> ***Overall performance can suffer
> when egotism drives decisions.***

6. HIRE THE BEST PEOPLE

Your team needs to be composed of the very best people you can hire or promote from within. If that means they are "better" than you, then hire them. Good leaders are never concerned about whether a subordinate could take their position. A good leader will become known for his pool of excellent employees. Remember, you cannot move up in an organization until there is someone capable of taking your place.

Thus, good leaders are never concerned about hiring people who are better, smarter, or more skilled. Leaders have confidence in their own abilities and keep their eyes on the purpose and mission of the organization. Leaders are rewarded for their ability to get a job done well.

Management knows that it was the team leader who hired the quality employees, trained them, managed them, and used them to achieve good results.

New leaders can come from all levels of the organization. Existing leaders should be constantly alert for employees who exhibit qualities of good leadership. It is the responsibility of leaders to find other people who can bring value to the organization or to their team.

Leadership development must be an ongoing process within the organization and in every team. The most successful organizations have outstanding leaders who develop other outstanding leaders and high performing team members.

7. DON'T MAKE IT PERSONAL

Good leaders do not personalize the words or actions of their team members or other detractors. Why? If leaders listened to every suggestion or complaint, they would never get their agenda off the ground. But they do need to hear good ideas and filter out the poor ones. This is not an easy task, but good leaders can do this with objectivity.

Leaders must understand that others have their own agendas and perceptions. They may even feel insecure and are seeking clarity about the leader's intentions in order to determine their own thinking. They may just want to contribute, have input, and feel part of the team. Good leaders are able to hear the input, filter out the bad, and not allow all the noise to get the work off track.

If you can check your feelings at the door and do not allow suggestions to feel like personal attacks, you are more likely to hear the good input from others. Listening well to this flow of information often can be the source of the first warning signs of underlying problems that should be addressed.

If you have a good filter you stand a better chance of making corrections or clarifying issues before they become serious problems. Misunderstandings can be fixed before they create serious roadblocks for your goals if you are listening well and with objectivity.

8. LEADERS ARE NOT ALWAYS RIGHT

Leaders are not perfect. Those who recognize they may be wrong about something have a much higher chance of long-term success. Leaders often have a much higher skill level, but that does not mean that their decisions are always right and cannot be improved. The most effective leaders are able to hear the suggestions or warnings that have merit. They will compare the input to reality, evaluate the situation, and make changes as appropriate.

Leaders are not infallible, even though some may think they are. Leaders do have flaws and the best leaders exercise great care in making decisions and listening to constructive feedback. The best leaders are decisive and do not modify their ways because someone else doesn't like their course of action. Good leaders will analyze the circumstances and make decisions after considering all the information available. They quickly admit wrong decisions and implement changes to correct mistakes.

9. ALL ABOARD!

Once an issue or question has been decided, everyone should be on board working toward the same purpose and goal. Disagreement and respectful argument is acceptable until a decision has been made. Once a decision is made, all leaders and team members should be working toward the desired end result, whether they agree with the decision or not.

In some organizations leaders will be fired or replaced if their disagreement with a decision is vocal or impacting progress toward the desired result. Unfortunately in some organizations disagreements are allowed to fester and create serious morale problems.

10. BE COURAGEOUS

Good leaders have the courage to make tough decisions for the good of the team and the organization. The right decisions may not be popular but good leaders stand firm because they know and understand the purpose and mission of both the team and the organization. Having the courage to make the right decision can be the difference between success and total failure.

11. NEVER LOSE FOCUS

Good leaders never lose focus of the mission or how the work of their team fits within the purpose of the organization. Good leaders set goals that are attainable, realistic, and timely. The focus is on the goals of the team that fit within the purpose and mission of the organization. When leaders or subordinates take their eye off the goal, it is easy to lose focus and be influenced by unimportant or unrelated issues.

Leaders with a mindset for growth are continually looking for ways to advance the goals of the organization. The environment may change but good leaders never lose focus on growing and improving their organization. Thus, there is an emphasis on technology, efficiency, and communication. If you want to be better than the competition you cannot lose sight of the basics.

12. THE CUSTOMER IS #1

Successful companies will have a primary focus on the customer. If you cannot make your customers happy or satisfied, long-term success is highly unlikely. New companies must have an absolute obsession with pleasing and satisfying customer needs. The trust of the customer is paramount and all actions and decisions must account for the needs and desires of the customers buying or using the organization's products or services.

This means that customer satisfaction must be a core value of the organization. There is no business without customers. Nothing can happen in an organization until a customer buys something. They are the life blood of the organization. They are the reason the company exists. If the focus of the organization ever moves away from the customer, the ultimate success of the company will be in jeopardy.

TIPS YOU COULD USE

a. Underline, circle, or highlight the 1 to 3 techniques above that you think could make the most impact if you implemented them in your life or career. You will revisit these choices at the end of the book in the Planning section.

If you were to adopt one or two of these techniques, which ones would you choose?

1. Wisdom

2. Innovation
3. Excellence
4. Simple
5. No egotism
6. Best people
7. Personal
8. Being right
9. All aboard
10. Courageous
11. Focus
12. Customer #1

b. There may be other things you think would make a difference. Write them below:

_____

_____

_____

_____

CONCLUSION

Is any one of these techniques absolutely necessary to be an outstanding leader? Possibly not! But any of them might be extremely useful depending on the nature of the organization. You should examine these techniques and determine which ones might be particularly useful in your situation.

If the customer is not the number one focus of your organization, you should determine why and ask the question, "What would happen in this organization if the number one focus was on the customer?"

If your organization does not have a desire to hire and train the *very best employees*, you must ask why.

Lastly, if your organization is not innovative, you should examine your competitors and determine how important innovation is in your industry. Is there any chance that your organization could be overwhelmed by change during the next several years? What product or system needs to be the focus for innovation in order to stay competitive?

Wisdom to Action Challenge

Audit your inner circle: Are there voices that consistently challenge or elevate you? If not, reach out to someone who inspires growth. If yes, empower one team member this week to lead a project beyond their comfort zone—then step back and observe their growth.

Chapter 8
TIPS: Be a Better Leader

*You become a better leader because you
want to become a better leader!*

If you Google "effective leadership skills," or "characteristics of a good leader," the suggestions given are usually focused on overcoming some weakness in order to become a better leader. If the weakness is really bad, the suggestion may have some merit, but being a better leader is not necessarily about fixing weaknesses.

Good leaders maximize their strengths rather than become overly concerned about fixing weaknesses. Self-awareness and self-discipline are very important characteristics for people who want to be good leaders.

We have covered a number of important characteristics of good leaders in previous chapters. You may note that we have not discussed "leadership styles." That's because we are more focused on practical results and the principles and qualities of leadership than on spending time identifying "styles." Regardless of your style you must use the principles, qualities, and traits discussed herein to be an effective leader.

This book is not about an academic analysis of leadership theories or styles, but an attempt to help you develop better leadership skills. Our purpose is not to discuss or analyze your style or category of leadership. We want you to understand all the ways you can be a better leader and help you adopt those qualities and techniques that will improve your leadership abilities.

This chapter will not necessarily present any new information but will provide you with a brief discussion of some valuable practices you could implement to improve your leadership skills. They are all good suggestions but they may not necessarily all be important to you. Focus on those you believe would have the biggest impact on your leadership ability.

This chapter provides tips rather than a serious examination of the key aspects of leadership. We have covered the key issues in Chapters 3-7. This chapter will bring some new thoughts mixed in with some different aspects of subjects previously discussed.

If you are serious about improving your leadership skills, implement at least one of the following tips in your work environment this week.

MAKE MEETINGS PRODUCTIVE

Meetings can be a great waste of time for a leader if nothing substantial is being accomplished. Leaders must conduct their meetings efficiently and demand that their junior leaders do the same. Time is money, and a great deal of both can be wasted sitting in non-productive meetings. Several guidelines that can be followed to make meetings more productive include:

- start and end on time,
- no meetings should be scheduled for longer than one hour,
- the maximum number of attendees should be ten,
- there should be a written agenda, and
- those attending should expect to contribute or answer questions.

Time is a very valuable resource and it should not be wasted. Meetings should focus on the task at hand and not be allowed to wander into other areas of discussion. New or old topics should be on the agenda if they are to be discussed. Additional discussions might be added at the end of a meeting if the time has not expired. Respect your employees' time and end meetings at the scheduled time.

KNOW AND COMMUNICATE LIMITS

The best working environment exists when everyone knows the limits and expected working climate. That does not mean freedom is removed and curiosity is stifled. Simply establish standard operational procedures so that boundaries are clearly understood. For example:

- Don't assign work that subordinates cannot do.
- Don't allow teams to go beyond boundaries where they would be wasting time and money.
- Make sure that everyone knows and understands the necessary budget constraints.
- Make it clear when and why outside expertise may be required.

AVOID COMMON PITFALLS

Everyone makes mistakes! Even good leaders err. Some mistakes can be avoided and others not so much. Avoid the common ones so you have time to deal with new or challenging situations. Here are six common leadership mistakes:

1. Trying to do it all or make every decision.
2. Thinking you are smarter than others and you know all the answers.

3. Failing to remember employees are watching you all the time.
4. Trying to make everything about you and not the team or organization.
5. Failing to communicate clearly and concisely.
6. Being slow or reluctant in making decisions.

REVIEW MISTAKES

Many great leaders believe that they learned the most from correcting mistakes. Once a problem has occurred and been fixed or resolved, key members of the team should review the situation, learn why the mistake occurred, and communicate new procedures or guidelines that would prevent the error from recurring. Good leaders learn from errors and make sure that preventable mistakes are not repeated.

LEARN FROM THE PAST

History is a great teacher. Someone has said that "Everything has already happened. We are just repeating old mistakes." If we don't learn from past mistakes, shame on us. Both good and bad lessons are scattered across the landscape of history. There have been both spectacular success stories and humiliating failures. Studying great leaders of the past can be both interesting and profitable. Share with your team what you learn.

HAVE FUN

Great leaders make the work, the work environment, and the interpersonal relationships fun. Laughing together and with each other (not at each other) can be a great tension reliever. It allows employees to relax and provides a moment to refocus and recharge.

Some organizations have a game area where employees can go for a few minutes to think or talk about something other than work. It is also good for workers at desks to get up and move around each hour. Five minute breaks can be great stress relievers and allow employees to return to work with a new mindset.

UNDERSTAND THE YOUNGER GENERATION

Some massive changes have occurred in the nature of people during the past few years. The ability and nature of the younger generation to relate to others has been dramatically changed by technology and particularly the smart phone and social media. Many of the young generation leaders today have grown up in situations where their interaction with others is through technology, not face-to-face.

This interaction is constant in the sense that it can occur continually throughout the day by using texting and messaging systems. But most senior leaders and much of middle management in many companies do not communicate in this manner in their organizations. This can be a significant hurdle for many younger generation employees who have become relatively isolated because much of their social contact is through technology.

Leaders must be very aware of the possibility that younger employees may have inadequate people skills, below average social skills, and an inability to relate to others in a close team operational setting. Perceptive leaders will recognize these issues and spend time working with younger leaders to develop the necessary skills to be productive in the existing work environment.

ALLOW SUBORDINATES TO SHADOW YOU

My kids used to love to go to work with me because it gave them insight into what I did and inflated how important they thought I was. They told their friends about the experience and got a little puffed up. That same concept can work with your subordinates. Not only do they get a chance to rub elbows with people they would not normally work with, but they have the opportunity to talk to the boss about anything they want.

They gain a peek at what the leader is doing, how she does it, and even sometimes the problems she faces. It is quality time for the subordinate and it costs the leader almost nothing. Solid working relationships can be cemented for a lifetime from these experiences.

BALANCE YOUR FEEDBACK

Often much of the feedback from leaders is centered on problems, weaknesses, and improvements that must be made. If this is the entirety of the communication, it will be a pretty negative experience for everyone involved, including the team leader.

Every meeting or communication dealing with problems should also have some positive feedback in order to balance the conversation and encourage subordinates. Both negative and positive feedback will help employees grow and develop in their jobs. Constructive feedback is necessary but it is often far more effective when accompanied by some conversation related to what employees are doing well.

HONOR THE PAST

New leaders or new situations often require special interaction and communication to get the ball rolling in a new environment. It is always good to talk about past success and to honor those accomplishments. Not only does it encourage the employees but it also shows that you have done your homework and made the effort to know what the team had previously accomplished. Touching on the past and honoring former achievements will help build a bridge to the present.

New leaders, however, need to focus on the new team, not their own past personal achievements. Nothing is accomplished by leaders who brag about their old team. The leader's past accomplishments are not particularly of interest to the new team.

TELL THEM WHY

Good leaders will not only give clear and concise instructions concerning the work but they also explain why. "Just because I told you to do it," like you may use in frustration with your kids, won't do much to encourage cooperation with your subordinates. Employees don't always need to know why they are doing something, but such knowledge wisely communicated will indicate that the leader cares, trusts, is not hiding something, and wants cooperation and feedback.

Good leaders will provide both a general understanding of what is going on and adequate details about why the work is being done. This provides an opportunity for the team to make suggestions that could improve the work process. Sometimes employees can suggest major innovations when they understand the purpose of the work and why it is being performed.

RECOGNIZE GOOD WORK

When employees and team members do a good job, make sure everyone knows. Exceptional work might warrant a written note to the division boss or even the CEO. Employees deserve to be appreciated for work well done. Teams will draw together, team leaders will be admired, job satisfaction will rise, and employees will be motivated to do a better job, all because they know that if they do a good job they are appreciated.

THINK AND TALK ABOUT CHANGE

The one thing that is certain in the world of business is that there will be change. The relevant question is how capable are you, your team, and your organization in reacting to important change. Many people and organizations learned that in very abrupt and demanding ways during COVID.

If an organization is always thinking about change, new possibilities, and different systems, they will be prepared for change when it is either discovered or thrust upon them. Organizations can be transformed by change – both for the good and for the bad. Good leaders never cease looking for changes that can impact their business.

Frequently talking about change, participating in workshops about new technologies, or doing team exercises focused on a new environment can prepare a team for real change when it happens. Change can be frightening, but if you have been preparing for it, it won't be so daunting when it occurs.

WORK TOGETHER

Leadership and the organization must be on the same page and heading in the same direction in order to achieve common goals. It is not effective to have everyone trying to reach the mountaintop but have multiple teams trying to get there on their own.

It is far more effective if everyone is working together, helping each other, using common resources, and sharing information. The road is long and resources are often limited. When everyone is on the same road going the same direction the possibilities for success are increased.

IT'S NOT ABOUT YOU

Unless you are the owner of the company the work and goals are not about you. In most organizations the focus should be on the purpose and mission of the organization. Leaders must align their words and actions to promote and advance the goals of the organization. Subordinates should not be confused about the priorities because a leader makes himself more important than the business.

BE GOAL FOCUSED BUT MISSION CONTROLLED

If you take your eye off the goals things will not go well. Energy and planning must be directed at the work at hand or the team will suffer consequences. If your energy is not focused on the mission of the organization, serious repercussions can go up the chain of command.

KNOW STRENGTHS AND WEAKNESSES

Identify the team member's strengths and weaknesses and organize the work to maximize the quantity and quality of the work. Team members should be spending most of their time utilizing the skills and abilities that are strengths. Teams should be formed with all the necessary skills so that the weaknesses of one member are covered by the strengths of another.

TIPS YOU COULD USE

a. Underline, circle, or highlight the 1 to 3 tips above that you think could make the most impact if you implemented them in your life or career. You will revisit these choices at the end of the book in the Planning section.

b. There may be other things that you think would make a difference. Write them below:

_____

_____

_____

_____

"Leadership is the capacity to translate vision into reality."
Warren G. Bennis[38]

Wisdom to Action Challenge

Identify a recurring friction point in your team. Instead of solving it yourself, host a collaborative session where others propose solutions. Reflect: How did empowering others shift the dynamic? What did you learn about humility and shared purpose?

Chapter 9
Practical Decision-Making

"Unintended consequences rush us recklessly through life, allowing no time for perspective."
(Unknown)

Special note to reader: *This chapter is duplicated in the free PDF and 99 cent eBook we provide in the free PDF copy ("Wise Decision-Making") – see ad pages at the beginning of this book. Additional information is provided in the PDF and eBook compared to what we have included here. Therefore if this subject is particularly interesting to you, pick up one of these copies.*

We feel that decision-making is a key leadership trait and deserves particular attention. The PDF and eBook copies are more focused on making personal life choices. Here the focus is on business decisions.

MAKING SOUND DECISIONS

1. Introduction

Many of us give this subject little attention, even though it's a very important leadership skill. Making good decisions is not that hard if we think through the reasonable alternatives. Unfortunately, we often do not spend adequate time thinking! Can we always get it right? No! But, we can significantly improve the process

One of the biggest reasons leaders struggle in making decisions is fear. You may have fear of the unknown, failure, or missing out on something better. We must not allow these fears to paralyze us. Making *no* decision may be the worst choice we can make.

Leaders who are focused on goals are less likely to make wrong or poor decisions. Why? They have the advantage because they are thinking about their decisions and are aware of the potential consequences of such choices.

There are times when we are presented with choices that could ultimately create major problems in our work lives. Opportunities for bad decisions are all around us. Making decisions is an important part of being a leader.

2. The Academics of Decision-Making

Most standard textbooks on the subject of decision-making condense the process down to several key steps. For example:

> **Clarify the Issue:** What is the problem? How can it be identified or described? What is the real issue?

> **Gather the Data:** Before you can do anything you must gather relevant data and information about the issue from all available sources.

> **Possible Alternatives:** What are the reasonable actions that might be taken to resolve the issue? What are the viable alternatives? What will the alternatives produce? How risky are these options?

> **Best Choice:** Which alternatives produce the best risk/reward solutions for the organization? Select the best alternative given your situation.

> **Implement:** Implement your choices.

> **Monitor:** Regularly review your progress.

These are the basic steps in making most decisions.

The key to any method is to approach the problem in an organized manner and logically consider the actions that might be taken. Then choose the best one for you given your situation and the organization's penchant for risk.

We can make decisions in a number of different ways. Sometimes it's simply instinct or intuition. We just know or feel what the right thing is to do. Others gather data and information, filling notebooks with everything they can think of that would help determine the right choice. Some of us make a check list of questions and answers before we decide. Another approach is to ask every trusted person you know to weigh in on the decision. Finally, there is the trusted "pros and cons" approach.

We have chosen an analytical approach for making business decisions. It requires looking at a number of different issues before making a decision. Some of these issues and questions may not apply to every question or to your particular situation. Just ignore those and focus on the questions that are pertinent.

3. Short and Sweet

For those of you who must make this process short and sweet, the following three questions may be adequate for you to make a good decision.

> a. Should the organization do it or not do it? Why?
> b. What are the detailed pros and cons?
> c. What is the best alternative given the pros and cons?

There is really nothing wrong with the "short and sweet" method, but we do not recommend it for serious business decisions. The key in this method is identifying all the important pros and cons. If you are not sure you have thought of everything, then consider the more detailed questions later in this chapter and determine if anything comes to mind that would change how you might proceed.

4. Experience

Your previous experience and the experience of others can be invaluable in making good decisions. Often you can avoid mistakes by learning from the experience of someone else. Find a trusted experienced person who likely could help and ask their opinion. For example, talk to a retired manager or supervisor from your area.

The experienced person may have experience in what you are facing. If you are considering starting or buying a business it would be helpful to get advice from someone who runs his own business. There may be pitfalls or rewards you know nothing about. This concept is true for many decisions – find someone who has already experienced the problem and found a solution.

5. Tips For Being a Good Decision-Maker

a. **Warning: Don't be overconfident.** Be confident but never assume every idea will work. Don't look at everything through rose colored glasses.

b. **Time-frame.** Make sure you think about both the short-term and long-term impact of your decisions. Something that is very good in the short term may be very bad in the long term.

c. Importance. Know the importance of the decision in the overall scheme of things. Don't waste time on a decision that has no real value. Assign a dollar value if that is possible. What are the potential good or bad results that cannot be easily measured?

d. Analysis of situation. Look at your situation from different viewpoints. Don't lock yourself into just one frame of reference. From what different viewpoints might you consider the issues and what are the impacts? Ask yourself what would happen if you did the opposite of what you are considering. What would happen if you did nothing at all?

e. Think about it. Make sure you take adequate time to fully consider the issues and your proposed solutions. But don't overthink it. If you begin to overthink the question you can end up going down a lot of time-consuming and irrelevant rabbit trails. It is easy to lose focus if you continually review the same material again and again.

f. Prioritize. Every decision you make should be measured against organizational values, priorities, or goals. Make sure you know what is important. Don't waste time and effort considering changes that have very little importance.

g. The wrong problem. Sometimes it is easy to misdiagnose the situation. Have you correctly identified the problem? Do you know what is happening and why, or are you just guessing?

h. Evaluate the risk. Make sure you know the real underlying risks you are taking. Who or what will be impacted by your choices and how will they be affected? Compare what could be lost against what could be gained. Is the risk worth it? What happens if the situation must be abandoned? What could you do up front to reduce the risk?

i. Extremes. Be reasonable in projecting into the future. Examine any history that is available. Is a good middle-of-the-road approach a viable choice? Beware of the extremes.

j. Advisors and mentors. We all have trusted friends, mentors, and advisors whom we could ask for feedback. Get their advice, but understand that in the end, you must make the decision. This is not a committee taking a vote. You are responsible.

k. Core values. Never violate your core values. Don't even consider something that would compromise your standards. If you have a sense that you are doing something wrong, stop and consider what is really going to happen if you proceed. Don't allow anger, fear, feelings, or emotions to convince you to do something that you would regret.

l. Information. You need information and data in order to make good decisions. You cannot even begin thinking about solutions until you know the facts. Make sure that the data you gather is valid and applicable to your situation.

m. Instincts. Sometime instincts are valid but most of the time they are not good ways to make decisions. Instinct may work if you are seasoned in the subject at hand and have made successful decisions in this area in the past.

n. Fear. Fear of making a mistake or of incurring bad consequences can sometimes prevent people from making any decision at all. Don't freeze up worrying about all the possible consequences. Get help. Get advice. Get moving. Don't be paralyzed.

o. Reasonable alternatives. Limit the options you are considering to those that have a reasonable chance of success. That will usually be 2 to 4 possibilities. Recheck your thinking and move forward with the best alternative available. If a better solution is identified at a later time, make the necessary changes to improve the situation. There is nothing wrong with changing your mind if a better solution becomes evident.

p. Focus. Stay focused on the problem. Keep your eye on the issue at hand. Don't become distracted and try to solve some other problem. Know what you want to achieve and focus on that result.

q. Emotions. Don't allow emotions to sway your decisions because the result could be disastrous. On the other hand, don't totally ignore them either. Understand the role emotions play in your personal decision-making process.

r. Break down big decisions. It is usually easier to make a number of small decisions than one really big one. If you are faced with a big and presumably serious decision, break it down into its component parts. It is much easier to make smaller decisions that accumulate into one big one than to tackle the entire problem.

s. Cost. Ask yourtself what this decision will cost in dollars, relationships, or missed opportunities. Know the cost of <u>not</u> making a decision (which is a decision itself). Cost should be part of your risk/reward evaluation.

t. Impact. What is going to happen? What other events will be set into motion? What will others think about the value of this decision? Will you get support or criticism?

u. Thinking versus doing. Don't spend all your time thinking. At some point the thinking must turn into doing. Spend adequate time thinking and analyzing the situation. When there is nothing more to think about, it is time for a decision.

v. Slow speed ahead. Implement your solutions slowly enough that you know what is working and what is not. Give your solutions time to succeed or fail. Don't rush to judgment. Don't try to implement too much too fast such that you lose control of the situation.

w. Change direction if necessary. You can never know in advance or be sure that a particular decision will be correct. There is some risk in every alternative. Be prepared to take risks, and be prepared to fix problems or change direction if the results dictate the solution is not working.

x. Mistakes. Don't worry about making mistakes. Everyone makes them, and they often occur at the most inopportune times. When they occur, the focus should be on fixing the problem, not on casting blame.

y. Stay the course. Once you have made your decision, stick with it unless you have clear evidence that you are on the wrong path. Don't change your mind because you get cold feet or have a bout of anxiety.

z. Timing. Poor timing can make some decisions very difficult to implement or achieve. If you are dealing with a timing situation, re-evaluate your options to stop, slow down, or go forward.

> *"You are free to choose, but the choices you make today will determine what you have, be, and do in the tomorrow of your life."*
> Zig Ziglar[39]

TIPS YOU COULD USE

a. Underline, circle, or highlight the 1 to 3 tips above that you think could make the most impact if you implemented them in your life or career. You will revisit these choices at the end of the book in the Planning section.

b. There may be other things that you think would make a difference. Write them below:

_____

_____

_____

_____

TEN DETAILED STEPS TO GOOD DECISIONS

1. DEFINE IT: Obtain _all_ the necessary information and state the question or problem in a simple, understandable, clear sentence or two.

    a. Gather the information necessary to make the decision. Know the facts and the history. You will never get 100% of the information – 80% is pretty good.

    b. Know the timeline and time requirements of the decision.

    c. What is the _real_ problem or issue? Define it correctly and completely. What do you have to decide?

    d. Don't avoid or ignore any facts. Do your homework and research well.

    e. Define the problem, opportunity, or decision. Write it down for clarity and perspective.

2. LEGAL or ETHICAL: Does this decision involve any legal issues, ethical standards, moral boundaries, or company rules and policies? Clarify in detail.

    a. Would it violate society's laws or the organization's core values or policies?

    b. Is this a question of right versus wrong or pushing ethical boundaries in any way? Explain.

    c. Will the organization be proud of the outcome?

3. CONSEQUENCES: What are the consequences? Can I live with them? Who and what will be affected, influenced, or impacted?

    a. What is the impact on my team and the organization? Does this create unreasonable expectations for me or others?

    b. Will this decision help or hurt the team or the

organization in any way?

c. Will this decision or solution change lives? How?

d. How will this feel in 6 months, in 12 months, in 24 months?

e. What is the short and long-term impact? Am I likely to make the same decision if I wait two weeks or two months?

f. If I can't please everyone, who must I please in this situation?

   Co-workers - Friends - Organization - Investors

g. Count the cost! Just because it feels right or seems like the thing to do, it may not fit with the time schedule, available resources, or skills of team members

4. FINANCIAL RISKS and REWARDS: What are the risks and rewards? What can we gain or lose? Are the risks reasonable?

a. What resources do I need – particularly those I do not already have? Can I acquire the necessary resources at a reasonable cost?

b. What is the worst case scenario? How likely is it? Could I live with that? Can the organization afford to lose what is invested?

c. Am I being realistic?

5. EXPERTISE: Do I have the knowledge, skill, and wisdom to make this decision?

a. Do I need additional wisdom, advice, skill, information, or experience to make this decision?

b. Do I have or can I obtain the necessary expertise and resources to accomplish this goal or project?

c. Who should be making this decision? Is it me or somebody else?

d. Do I have the authority to make this decision?

6. ADVISORS: Seek out advisors to provide intelligent and honest advice.

    a. Seek out <u>trusted</u> advisors who are trustworthy, capable, intelligent, and diverse; who have my interests at heart, and are not "yes" men.

    b. <u>Listen</u> (really listen) to their advice. What do they think? What is their counsel? What is their logic and reasoning?

    c. Do my friends and advisors agree or are they divided or conflicting? Why? What's the issue?

    d. Don't permit the advisors to make the decision! Advisors may have their own or a different agenda!

7. CONSIDERATIONS: Is it consistent with my core values and the values of the organization? Are my motives right? Am I being influenced by feelings, emotions, fears, or insecurities?

    a. CORE VALUES:
- Does this conflict with the organization's core values or policies in any way?
- Is it just and fair (right)?

    b. GOALS:
- How does this fit with the organization's short and long-term business goals?

    c. PASSION:
- What emotions are impacting this decision? They should not override good judgment!

    d. MOTIVES:
- What are my motives? Do I have any hidden agendas? Am I trying to fool myself?
- Are there selfish or unworthy ambitions involved? Is pride or arrogance present?
- Am I doing something for the wrong reasons?

e. FEELINGS:
- Feelings may be very deceptive and can lead to undesirable results.
- Do not be influenced by the age-old concept of "I feel good about it."

f. FEARS:
- What are my inherent fears and how are they influencing my decision?
- Fears cannot be allowed to dictate decisions, but they must be evaluated.
- Do I feel pressured? What is that pressure?

8. ALTERNATIVE SOLUTIONS: Take time to fully analyze the information in order to make a fully informed decision from several viable alternatives.

a. Analyze the information and develop all <u>viable</u> solutions.

b. Think outside the box. Expand the solutions. Look at the problem from a different viewpoint.

c. Reduce the options down to the 2 most viable alternatives.

9. DECIDE: Verify the facts and consider the solution, then make the decision.

a. VERIFY: Verify the facts as necessary. Confirm the opinions of your advisors and settle in for some thinking.

b. SIMPLIFY: Make it simple. Don't make it more complicated than it already is.

c. THINK: Think about the solution. Spend time evaluating the tough issues surrounding this decision. Don't allow problems or unknowns to frustrate you or emotionally drain you. Big decisions are hard work!

d. TIME: How much of my time will be required? Can we do this in the required time-frame?

e. RIGHT: Is it fair, equitable, and just? By this point you should have eliminated anything that is illegal, violates core values, or is against your company's rules and polices.

f. ANALYSIS PARALYSIS: Don't overthink it. Don't be afraid to make a decision. If the result ends up being wrong, then accept the mistake, correct it, and move on.

g. ADVISORS: Would others (my advisors) in my situation make the same decision? Why? Why not?

h. SOCIAL MEDIA: How will social media react to this decision? Do I need to be ready to respond? Do I care?

i. RUSH: If I am being _forced_ to make an immediate answer or choice, then the answer should probably be NO!

j. SUSTAINABLE: Is the decision a permanent solution? Will I be facing the same issues again in several months?

k. SAYING NO: It's okay to say no! If it's not right, it's not right.

l. DELAY: Not making a decision is a decision. No decision is choosing the status quo.

m. PERFECT DECISIONS: There is no such thing as a perfect decision. Are you generally comfortable and content with your decision? If not, more study and analysis may be necessary, or the answer may be "no."

n. DECIDE: Decide and move forward.

10. AFTERWARD: Now that the decision is made, monitor the situation closely so that the intended result occurs. Take corrective action as needed.

a. How will I monitor the results? How will I know if there are problems?

b. Who do I go to with questions or problems if difficulties arise?

c. Doubts are common. Make sure they are valid. Don't ignore them, but don't let them get out of hand. Don't allow problems or difficulties to automatically raise doubts.

TIPS YOU COULD USE

a. Underline, circle, or highlight the 1 to 3 decision-making concepts above that you think could make the most impact if you implemented them in your life or career. You will revisit these choices at the end of the book in the Planning section.

b. There may be other things that you think would make a difference. Write them below:

_____

_____

_____

_____

CONCLUSION

Some organizations may want their leadership characteristics weighted very highly on results. Leaders may have to deliver results in order to survive – like football coaches. Others may need leaders to be more hands-on with daily operations. Thus, the leaders must know the details of every job within the team's operations.

It may be desirable for leaders to have a strong budgeting and financial background, particularly if expenses are critical to successful operations. Thus financial management and cost monitoring become critical activities of the leader.

"Immature poets imitate; mature poets steal; bad poets deface what they take, and good poets make it into something better, or at least something different."
T.S. Eliot[42]

Wisdom to Action Challenge

Before your next significant decision, pause. Write down the core issue, potential risks, and how the choice aligns with your long-term goals. After acting, revisit your notes: Did clarity reduce hesitation? What lessons emerged for future decisions?

Chapter 10 – Planning
Part 1: Life Analysis

———

LEADERSHIP LIFE PRINCIPLE:
Lead well and be a loyal follower.

INTRODUCTION

The objective of this Life Analysis chapter is to survey your life situation for information that will be used in later chapters to identify your *personal* core values, life priorities, commitments, and goals. In Chapter 13 we will formulate action steps to improve your leadership skills.

If you have already read one of the other books in this Series and completed the Life Analysis in that book, the questions and exercises are the same, but, your answers concern a different subject. Some of your responses will be the same or similar and you might want to have that book handy as you complete this Life Analysis.

Most of us have never done an extensive self-examination and probably have not written down the results. I can tell you personally there is much to be gained from writing them down rather than just thinking, talking, or meditating about them. It will give you a clear picture of your life and help you evaluate what you really want to accomplish.

The focus of this book is to address <u>one</u> particular topic in your life. It is not a complete life plan. A complete and detailed Life Plan is the subject of our *Life Planning Handbook*. See the "Next Steps" page at the end of this book for more information.

Our life planning process has five primary parts which we will cover in the following chapters.

Chapter 10, Part 1 – Life Analysis: What is your life situation today?
Chapter 11, Part 2 – Life Values: What is important to you?
Chapter 12, Part 3 – Life Principle Goals: What are your objectives?
Chapter 13, Part 4 – Action Steps: How do you get from where you are today to your goals?
Chapter 14, Part 5 – Ongoing Progress Review: How are you doing?

Planning is not a difficult process. It will certainly be easier for those who have thought about these questions before. You might even have an existing plan of some kind. If so, this will be a good check on where you are and how you are doing. If you have a plan, it would be worthwhile pulling it out as you progress through the remaining parts of this book.

> *"If you don't know where you're going,*
> *any path will get you there!"*
> unknown

I don't know the source of the quote above but I have had it emblazoned in my brain since my college days. I think it came from one of my college business classes or textbooks. I've heard it repeated a number of times over the years, probably because it is so true!

If you don't know your destination, then any choice of roads at all the forks in life will be an acceptable choice. It won't really matter which road you take because you don't have a destination in mind anyway. And when you get there you won't know you have arrived.

We need a purpose, a destination, and priorities so we are not wandering aimlessly through life. Even if you are not a "planning person," be assured we will walk you through each step.

Without purpose and direction it is difficult to make good choices. Just thinking about the questions we will ask in the following process will be helpful. Our planning process should produce these positive results:

- it will create focus, attention, and desire,
- it will cause action – doing something,
- it will begin to establish the importance of what you believe,
- it will help you make better decisions,
- it will help reduce distractions and hindrances, and
- it will motivate you.

"If your actions create a legacy that inspires others to dream more, learn more, do more and become more, then, you are an excellent leader."
Dolly Parton[41]

LIFE ANALYSIS – KNOW YOURSELF

The first step in any form of planning is to know and understand where you are today. What is your current situation? What is impacting your decisions and ultimately your life today? The first objective will be to identify your present situation and circumstances. Before we begin, take note of the following suggestions:

1. During this process you may find that you draw a blank on a particular question. If that happens, move on to the next question and return to the unanswered ones at a later time.

2. These questions relate specifically to the Leadership Life Principle which is focused on leading well. If that limited scope makes it difficult to answer any particular question, then answer from a broader life perspective if you think it would be helpful. If a question doesn't apply in any significant way, leave it blank.

3. You might find it convenient to write your initial responses In a separate notebook or computer and transfer that information to this book after you have thought about it and modified it to accurately reflect your thoughts and circumstances. Regardless of how you develop your answers, keep your notes, as they may be useful at a later date.

4. Remember, you are developing a plan focused on the Leadership Life Principle, not on your life in

general. Therefore, your responses should be focused on that subject.

KNOW YOURSELF – Interests

INSTRUCTION: What are the things and activities you love to do? What gives you satisfaction related to the Leadership Life Principle?

1.

_____

2.

_____

3.

_____

4.

_____

5.

_____

KNOW YOURSELF – Skills

INSTRUCTION: What are your greatest physical or mental skills and abilities related to the Leadership Life Principle?

1.

_____

2.

_____

3.

_____

4.

_____

5.

_____

KNOW YOURSELF – Strengths

INSTRUCTION: What are your strengths, special skills, and passions in regard to the Leadership Life Principle?

1.

_____

2.

_____

3.

_____

4.

_____

5.

_____

KNOW YOURSELF – Weaknesses

INSTRUCTION: What are your weaknesses in regard to the Leadership Life Principle?

1.

_____

2.

_____

3.

_____

4.

_____

5.

_____

KNOW YOURSELF – Roadblocks

Who or what things do you fear the most? What are the roadblocks, distractions, and hindrances that might prevent you from improving your leadership skills in any way? Circle any that might apply and add your own in the empty boxes.

Disabilities	Failure	Bankruptcy	Divorce	Loss of job
Public speaking	Confrontation	War	Loss of friends	Peer pressure
Poor health	My boss	Guilt	No legacy	God
Time	Apathy	Relationships	Death	Family
Inability to stand firm	Immoral behavior	Unethical behavior	Lack of skills	Emotions or feelings
Fears and insecurities	Lack purpose in life	Lack of Core values	Lack of patience	Improper motives
Bad habits				

INSTRUCTION: Based on what you circled above, record any <u>serious</u> roadblocks or hindrances that could prevent you from improving your leadership skills. Indicate the reason they are roadblocks.

1.

_____

2.

_____

3.

_____

4.

_____

KNOW YOURSELF – Character

How would you evaluate your personal character? Do you have any serious character flaws (your religious friends might refer to these as sins)? If you have any serious character flaws in your life, you may need to deal with them in order to make real progress toward the Leadership Life Principle objective.

INSTRUCTION: Circle the positive traits which you lack and the existence of character flaws that might hinder your ability to achieve the Leadership Life Principle.

LACK OF POSITIVE CHARACTER TRAITS:				
Honesty	Kindness	Caring	Forgiving	Goodness
Hopeful	Humility	Dependable	Loving	Diligence
Respectful	Godly	Patient	Generous	Satisfied
Peace	Merciful	Trustworthy	Self-controlled	Thankful
Devout	Disciplined	Obedient	Gentle	Prudent
Sincerity	Fair/Just	Grateful		
EXISTING CHARACTER FLAWS:				
Bad language	Boastfulness	Gossip	Slanderous	Lying
Cheating	Stubbornness	Anger	Hostility	Fear
Foolishness	Mischievousness	Rebellion	Hypocrisy	Envy
Unruliness	Ingratitude	Pride	Immorality	Addictions
Jealousy	Bitterness	Hatred	Unforgiving	Shame
Respect	Revenge	Deceit	Vanity	

The above list is not exhaustive. If there are other issues you should add, write them in the empty boxes above.

INSTRUCTION: Review the issues you have identified and list below what could <u>seriously</u> hinder achieving the Leadership Life Principle. List the issue and how it would negatively impact your ability to achieve your objectives.

1.

_____

_____

2.

_____

_____

3.

_____

_____

KNOW YOURSELF – Conclusion

This concludes your information gathering.

The next step in the process of knowing yourself is to use this information to determine your core values, priorities, and commitments.

Chapter 11 – Planning
Part 2: Life Values

———

LEADERSHIP LIFE PRINCIPLE:
Lead well and be a loyal follower.

CORE VALUES

What are the standards by which you live? What values do you cherish? What do you believe in? What values will you absolutely not compromise or violate? The latter are your *core values*.

Self-assessment and full understanding of yourself and your environment must begin with identifying and knowing your core values. Core values are the principles, standards, or beliefs that are so important to you that you would not violate them under any conditions.

You do need to know what matters most to you. You need to know your ethical and moral standards. What issues or actions do you believe in so strongly that you would be deeply ashamed if you violated them? These are values and principles you believe in and live by, and to the best of your ability you will not forsake them. They represent who you really are. They are your core values.

If you love and seek intellectual improvement you might have a core value related to seeking and gaining

157

knowledge and wisdom. If you are a dedicated parent you probably have core values related to your children or parenting. If you are focused on your career you may have core values about communication, influence, loyalty, reputation, motivation, or teamwork.

Core values may change or become more or less important as you age and advance up the ladder in your organization.

You may be aware of several of your core values but you probably have never written them down. This exercise will be an important step in understanding what is important to you.

If this is a new subject for you, you might start by looking at all the topics on the "Next Steps" page (after Appendix C) and determine if any of those subjects represent core values for you. There are other subjects that might be appropriate for you to consider. For example: wisdom, influence, health, security, fitness, family, service, ethics, joy, relationships, moderation, balance, justice/injustice, addictions, laws, and safety.

Your core values should cover the things that are important to you. For example, you might have this statement as a core value: "I will always try to do what is right and I will teach my children to do what is right, even if it is uncomfortable." Or, you might have a core value related to money: "I will never spend more than I earn. I will pay off credit cards monthly." Core values related to your career might include:

- I will never be dishonest with superiors, co-workers, subordinates, vendors or customers.
- I will be diligent and a hard worker. I will do my work to the very best of my abilities

FINAL CORE VALUES

Develop these values based on a total life perspective, not just the Leadership Life Principle, and make them work for you. If you have never thought about this before, we recommend you begin with 5 to 8, but no more than 12. This is a critical step in this planning exercise, so spend sufficient time thinking and evaluating your final choices. Remember, core values are those values or standards that you will absolutely not compromise or violate.

INSTRUCTION: Develop your list of core values and record them here. We suggest you try to list twelve and then cut the list back to the best 5 to 8.

1. _____

2. _____

3. _____

4. _____

5. _____

6. _____

7. _____

8. _____

9. _____

10. _____

11. _____

12. _____

Do any of the core values you listed above relate to leadership? If not, do you need one? You may not, but don't leave it off because you overlooked the obvious. You may want to include one or more in order to give your objectives for the Leadership Life Principle more focus and importance at this time.

LIFE VALUES: Priorities (initial list)

Again, our perspective in this particular exercise is your total life, not just the Leadership Life Principle.

What are the things that are very important to you today? What are your life priorities? Where do you currently spend your money and your time? What do you spend your life doing and thinking about? For this initial list of priorities, ignore anything new that you may be considering relative to leadership. Record just your priorities today (the good and the bad).

If you do something daily or regularly, then it is probably a priority. If you average more than an hour a day doing something, it's also probably a priority. What do you regularly spend money on? Assuming you have a normal 8:00 – 5:00 job, what do you do in the evenings and on weekends?

You might have Life Priorities related to your spiritual life, the educational system where you live, the ethical standards of your friends, your health and diet, hobbies and activities, raising your children, your marriage, your times of relaxation, politics, volunteer service, your work ethic, saving money, immorality, your job or career, where you will live, or your personal growth.

INSTRUCTION: What are your actual top 6 to 12 life priorities today? Record them here based on a total life perspective.

1.

_____

2.

_____

3.

_____

4.

_____

5.

_____

6.

_____

7.

_____

8.

_____

9.

_____

10.

_____

11.

_____

12.

_____

ISSUES – URGENCY:

If you learned that you had only two years of life left, what impact would that have on your Life Priorities? How might they change?

_____

_____

_____

_____

_____

_____

ISSUES – SACRIFICES AND RISKS:

What new risks or sacrifices would you have to make in order to accomplish the Leadership Life Principle? Would that change your current Life Priorities?

_____

_____

_____

_____

_____

ISSUES – KNOWING YOURSELF:
Look back over the "Life Analysis – Know Yourself" and determine if there is anything that should change or be added to your Life Priorities.

_____

_____

_____

_____

_____

ISSUES – LIVING A BETTER LIFE:
Given a desire to adopt the Leadership Life Principle for your life, what new priorities would you need to adopt? Ask yourself what you must absolutely do in order to successfully be a good leader. What new priorities does that create and how would any existing priorities have to change?

_____

_____

_____

_____

_____

_____

_____

FINAL LIFE PRIORITIES

Prepare a complete list below of your new and revised total Life Priorities. Try to keep this list at 6 to 8, but no more than 12. You should intentionally include priorities that relate to the Leadership Life Principle.

1.
_____

2.
_____

3.
_____

4.
_____

5.
_____

6.
_____

7.
_____

8.
_____

9.
_____

10.
_____

11.
_____

12.
_____

LIFE COMMITMENTS

Are these Commitments the same as Life Priorities? No! Your Life Priorities identify the _things that are very important_ to you, while Life Commitments are _things you must do_ to make Life Priorities a reality in your life. Life Commitments are sometimes useful if they focus on areas where you have particular difficulties.

It's very possible that there are new commitments you must make that are not directly related to the Leadership Life Principle. For example, if your desire is to be honest you will also have to commit to being trustworthy, dependable, reliable, and loyal. If you want to be generous, then you can't love money. If you desire to guard your speech, then you cannot be out of control and let anger control your tongue. If you are going to be an outstanding leader you will need to deal with the dichotomies of leadership (see end of chapter 5).

The point of these examples is to demonstrate that if you are serious about the Leadership Life Principle, then there may be other related commitments necessary to be successful. You could have a commitment that says you are going to commit to being a good leader, but that doesn't really provide you with much help. If you have difficulty making decisions, then a commitment to make timely or better decisions becomes a more meaningful commitment. If your difficulty with leadership revolves around poor or ineffective communication, you could commit to improving your communication skills. Try to make your commitments specific enough that they will be useful to you.

The important concept to recognize is that the Leadership Life Principle may *automatically* require committing to one or more other behaviors and traits that are related to leadership and may become troublesome if not an area of focus.

Since Life Priorities inherently identify your objectives, examine those priorities and determine the related commitments that you must make in order to achieve each Life Priority. The focus should be on what you must commit to in order to achieve the Leadership Life Principle.

INSTRUCTION: List the traits, behaviors, qualities, or habits that you must manage or control in order for you to achieve the Leadership Life Principle (one or two words).

1. _____

2. _____

3. _____

4. _____

5. _____

6. _____

7. _____

8. _____

9. _____

10. _____

FINAL LIFE COMMITMENTS

INSTRUCTION: Based on the above, develop the Life Commitments you feel you should make in order to successfully achieve the Leadership Life Principle. These should be significant commitments, therefore, select the 4 to 8 that would really help you in being a better leader.

> *"There's a difference between interest and commitment. When you are interested in doing something, you do it only when it's convenient. When you're committed to something, you accept no excuses, only results."*
> Kenneth Blanchard[42]

1.

_____

_____

2.

_____

_____

3.

_____

_____

4.

_____

_____

5.

_____

_____

6.

_____

_____

7.

_____

_____

8.

_____

_____

Chapter 12 – Planning
Part 3: Life Goals

———

LEADERSHIP LIFE PRINCIPLE
Lead well and be a loyal follower.

*"Life takes on meaning when you become motivated,
set goals and charge after them
in an unstoppable manner."*
Les Brown[43]

Our goal is the Leadership Life Principle: *I will lead well and be a loyal follower.* A complete plan would have other goals, but in this book we are focused only on one goal: *leadership.*

If it would be useful for you, you may want to note or record other Life Goals you already have or you want to make given the material you have read in this book.

Life Goals are your objectives for the future. They are influenced by your Core Values, Priorities, and your Commitments.

LIFE GOALS

INSTRUCTION: We have entered the Leadership Life Principle goal, and you may list other personal goals, if you like.

1. *I will lead well and be a loyal follower*

OTHERS (for future use):

2. _____

3. _____

4. _____

5. _____

6. _____

"Your ability to discipline yourself to set clear goals, and then to work toward them every day, will do more to guarantee your success than any other single factor."
Brian Tracy[44]

Chapter 13 – Planning
Part 4: Action Steps

LEADERSHIP LIFE PRINCIPLE:
Lead well and be a loyal follower.

***If you want something to happen,
you will need to take action.***

INTRODUCTION

All the work in the previous chapters has given you a wealth of knowledge about where you are today and what you want to achieve in the future. You have even written it down. This is the point at which you actually take the step to determine what you are going to do about it.

As you think about what you need to do, include language that would allow you to measure your success or progress, if possible. Where appropriate, include the dates when you intend to begin and complete each step. The best action steps are those that can be measured, allowing you to easily evaluate your progress.

In most cases the Life Principle involved will dictate the nature of the action steps you will want to take. For example, if the goal is to lead well by communicating better, the action steps need to be directed toward specific issues that will improve your communication.

Think about specific situations in which effective communication is very important. You might begin by listing the recurring communications that are important in your situation, for example:

- Daily status.
- Weekly or monthly update.
- One-on-one counseling or instruction.
- Performance evaluations.

If your *primary concern* is the written daily – monthly – communications, then only develop action steps for better written communications.

When you develop your action steps, concentrate on the areas that cause you difficulty. Don't bother with areas where you don't really have a problem.

ACTION STEPS – FIRST DRAFT

Following is a list of subjects for developing your action steps. You can do all of them or just those that you expect will produce the results you want. Your ultimate objective is to end up with 4 to 6 action steps you intend to implement. You will have other actions (maybe a large number) on your initial list, but the ultimate goal is 4 to 6 good steps that you are confident will have a significant impact on achieving your objectives.

IMPORTANT: Produce as many good ideas as possible in this initial process. They may be useful at a later date.

ACTION STEPS – Initial List

INSTRUCTION: Do each of the following in order to produce an initial list of actions steps for achieving the Leadership Life Principle. After you produce this initial list you will consolidate and remove the ideas that are not on target. We suggest doing this initial list in a separate notebook or on your tablet or computer.

Step #1 – TIPS FOR IMPROVEMENT

You have actually done much of the work for utilizing the tips we have discussed. In chapters 2 through 9 we provided tips and ideas on how you might improve a particular trait. You were asked to highlight 1 to 3 suggestions you thought might work best for you and to list any other thoughts you had that would improve that trait.

Go back through the entire list of tips you chose and the ideas you added and select the ones you might actually want to use as action steps. Choose the ones that would have the most positive impact on your leadership skills. Choose the best 4 to 12 tips, and write them in the space below in any order. [The tips are located on pages 27, 71, 88, 106, 118, 129, 139, and 145].

TIPS:

1.

_____

2.

_____

3.

_____

4.

_____

5.

_____

6.

_____

7.

_____

8.

_____

9.

_____

10.

_____

11.

_____

12.

_____

CHOOSE THE BEST TIPS:

From the list above, choose the top 4 to 6 tips and list them in priority order:

1.

_____

2.

_____

3.

_____

4.

_____

5.

_____

6.

_____

Make one or more of these tips the first entries on your to your master list of Initial Action Steps.

Step #2 – IMPLEMENTATION TECHNIQUES

It will be helpful for you to think about implementation techniques before you begin determining your final action steps. These are techniques you can utilize to help you achieve your goals. You might automatically mentally use some of these concepts when you are developing and working your plan. But if they are not already second nature to you, they could be part of your action steps.

Be Intentional. If you are going to accomplish anything of value, change some part of your life, or achieve a goal, you will need both discipline and intentionality. Developing a plan and even writing down action steps will accomplish very little unless you actually follow through. You must be committed and disciplined, and intentionally implement your plans.

Be open to change. Change is occurring daily all around us. If we are rigid and not open to new ways and new ideas, it is often difficult to accept good advice. For example, how can new ways to communicate help you be a good leader?

Seek knowledge and understanding. We cannot afford to be ignorant. Those with skills and expertise can teach us much. Seek new understandings rather than remain in a rut because "that's the way it has always been done."

Seek help. Ask trusted friends or mentors for advice or assistance.

Maximize use of your strengths. If you are making significant changes, utilize your strengths to assist in your success. You are likely to be more successful if you use your existing strengths than your weaknesses.

Make good decisions. Much of our success in business occurs when we make right, good, and proper choices. If this has been difficult for you in the past, make this one of your action steps. Review Chapter 9, if necessary.

Review the "IMPLEMENTATION TECHNIQUES" above and determine which techniques might be effective for your purposes. Include those techniques as action steps on your initial list, as needed.

Step #3 – CHARACTER ISSUES

Look back over Chapters 10 and 11 and identify situations that will make your commitment to the Leadership Life Principle difficult to achieve. Also, think about actions that would make the Life Principle easier to achieve if they existed or were true. Then write out action steps that would advance your ability to be a good leader.

> 1. What personal characteristics in the "Life Analysis – Know Yourself" section do you need to modify in order to make improvements?
>
> 2. Think about the times or situations when you have not been an effective leader. Develop initial action steps that would prevent those situations from occurring or at least be under control in the future.

Step #4 – LIFE VALUES

What Life Values (core values, priorities and commitments) require action steps in order to achieve the Leadership Life Principle? Add them to your list.

Step #5 – WHAT IF I FAIL?

Do you need any action steps relative to what you will do if something fails? Think in advance what you will do if you have a temporary lapse or failure of some kind. For example, if your goal is good written communications, what will you do if you write a very confusing update or a puzzling set of instructions? A possible action step might be to make a list of the things that were confusing and see if there is any common theme. You might ask three of your subordinates to list things that were confusing and explain what they didn't understand.

If you don't add an action step for possible failures, at a minimum you should think about the possible negative situations that might occur and know what you are going to do if they happen.

Step #6 – BRAIN STORMING

If you aren't satisfied with your list, try to think of other options. If you can't do that on your own, get a few friends to help you brainstorm the topics on which you need more input. The purpose here is to accumulate ideas, not evaluate them. You can do the evaluating later. Seek any kind of ideas! Often one seemingly crazy idea leads to a very good one.

Step #7 – CULL AND CONSOLIDATE

You should have a substantial list of steps and ideas after doing all of the above. Now it's time to finalize your initial list.

1. Reduce the list to the <u>good</u> and <u>workable</u> ideas. Remove anything you do not want to keep on your list.

2. Eliminate or combine the duplicates into similar groupings or headings.

3. Consolidate the similar ideas into one. You may want to have sub-points for the larger ideas.

4. Prioritize the groups. Within each group, prioritize the ideas.

5. Save this list permanently.

EXAMPLES

Your list might include statements like:

> a. I will have a friend or associate proofread all my written communications during the next 3 months before I send them out.
>
> b. I will not make quick decisions, but will follow a specific process in solving problems.
>
> c. I will take courses to improve my leadership skills.

d.   I will develop a written plan for each of my key subordinates to improve their job skills or develop their leadership abilities.

e. I will set or update job performance requirements that will improve the performance results of our team. My goal for our team is EXCELLENCE!

f. I will improve my motivation skills. I will learn what inspires my subordinates and learn how to better motivate others to higher levels of performance and organizational loyalty.

g. I will improve my understanding of the technology used in my section or division. I will begin a regular schedule of activities that will improve my understanding of significant changes that might impact the work of the organization and my team.

PLANNING ADVICE

Leadership is one of those abilities that involves a number of different skills melded together to achieve excellence. It's like being a good carpenter. No one becomes known for his skills because he is good at cutting boards straight. He must have a number of excellent woodworking skills to have a reputation as a good carpenter.

That is also the case with leadership. People who are elevated to lead others tend to have a number of skills and abilities that contribute to their reputation as leaders.

Therefore, leaders typically have strong self-discipline, focus, and high energy. They are not people who shy away from work, challenges, or conflict. They are sincere, genuine, and they don't give up.

Good leaders also are open to suggestions. They are not rigid. They will take an honest look at themselves and their environment and undertake most challenges, unless they know that they are not qualified. Thus, they have the ability to take an honest look at themselves and know their own strengths and weaknesses.

The best leaders are also humble and will put the needs of others on a level with their own needs. If you want to be a good leader commit to honestly evaluating your own capabilities and develop plans to improve those abilities.

Key to Success.

As we have indicated earlier in the book we feel that good communication and problem-solving skills are two of the most import traits for being a good or excellent leader. However there are other very important traits.

We believe that the key to success in acquiring the traits of a good leader are perseverance and commitment. This may mean that you must be bold in undertaking a plan to be an excellent leader. Of course, you must have a real desire to be a good leader. If you have that, and a reasonable amount of ability, then you simply need perseverance. Make it a personal challenge to be steadfast in your desire to be a good leader, no matter what setbacks occur.

Remain committed to your goal to be the best no matter what people say or how difficult it might seem. Nothing worthwhile is necessarily easy. Pursue excellence.

FINAL ACTION STEPS

SUBJECT: **LEADERSHIP**

GOAL: **To lead well and be a loyal follower.**

FINAL ACTION STEPS:

Choose the 4 to 6 best action steps from your initial list and enter them below

1.

_____

_____

_____

2.

_____

_____

_____

3.

_____

_____

_____

4.

_____

_____

_____

5.

_____

_____

_____

6.

_____

_____

_____

Consider entering reminders on your phone or computer.

REVIEW

Before you finalize your Action Steps, you should step back and take a broader look at what you have prepared.

1. CORE VALUES & PRIORITIES: Are your action steps consistent with your core values and revised life priorities?

_____

_____

2. PERSONAL COMMITMENT: Are your action steps consistent with your personal desires and commitments? Are you ready to make these changes in your life? Are you missing anything important?

_____

_____

Go back and modify your plans, if necessary.

GETTING STARTED

If you are ready to begin, go for it! Begin with any or all of the above action steps.

But if you have any fear or reluctance, start slowly. There is absolutely no reason to try to do everything at once. Choose the action step that you think will be the easiest to achieve and get started. When that is implemented, choose the next easiest action step, and proceed through the list in that manner.

Some people may have a preference to do the most difficult one first and get that out of the way. That's fine if that works for you. But if this is going to create significant change or stress in your life, we recommend you start slowly.

Chapter 14 – Planning
Part 5: Review

Ongoing Evaluation

LEADERSHIP LIFE PRINCIPLE:
Lead well and be a loyal follower.

"The life which is unexamined is not worth living."
Socrates[45]

FREQUENCY:

During the first eight weeks, review your plans weekly. In fact, as long as you have a significant list of action steps to accomplish you should take time weekly to evaluate your progress. At some point you can move to every two weeks and then monthly. As long as you still have things you want to implement, you should review your plan monthly.

We recommend you put this review time on your calendar and allow 90 minutes for your first review and update. Based on the time needed for your first review you can schedule future reviews.

SUCCESS:

Review your plan for success and failure. What can you discontinue, what should you add, and what have you achieved? Think particularly about your goals and priorities. How are you doing? Are you making progress?

MODIFICATION:

What can be removed because it has been successfully implemented? What is not working? What needs to be changed? What other action steps or ideas did you set aside when you developed your initial list? Should any of these ideas be added you your plan?

Check List

If you like to use check lists in completing tasks we have included one in Appendix B that lists all the steps in completing your Plan.

Chapter 15

Hope & Encouragement

What you place your hope in
will define the path for your life.

General

In "*Animal Dreams*" Barbara Kingsolver writes, "*The very least you can do in your life is figure out what you hope for. And the most you can do is live inside that hope. Not admire it from a distance but live right in it, under its roof.*"[66]

Hope is a very important component of our existence. You may not always be conscious of your hope, but it's what drives you forward; it is the inherent desire of your heart. It is often masked by other mental or emotional baggage, but it is there nevertheless.

Kingsolver's point is that we need to unmask that hope, embrace it, and intentionally bring it into our lives. We must not just think about it or admire it, but make it a part of our lives. Why? Because what we hope for will define the course of our lives. It defines what is ultimately important to us and it will shape our priorities.

What do you hope for?

MERRIAM-WEBSTER's definition of hope is to desire, with the expectation of obtaining the object of that desire. Genuine hope is not wishful thinking, but a firm assurance about things that are "unseen" and still in the future.

Hope looks ahead to a future expectation that is uplifting or optimistic. The opposite of hope is depression, sadness, or dejection. We can have different hopes for the many parts of our lives. Some are little hopes and others are large. Some may be huge. Lives can be built and lost on the nature of our hope.

What are your hopes? Take a few minutes before you proceed to think about and identify some of your hopes. What do you hope for? What hope sustains you? Are you conscious of your hopes? What hope would sustain you if you were living in dire circumstances? Jot down some notes about your thoughts on "hope:"

_____

_____

_____

_____

_____

_____

_____

"Loyalty is what makes us trust.
Trust is what makes us stay.
Staying is what makes us love,
and love is what gives us hope."
Glenn van Dekken[67]

The Result of Hope

Many wise sayings about hope indicate that righteous people hope for joy or happiness but the destiny of wicked people is misery. What does it mean that the righteous hope for joy? Why joy? What is joy? Someone with joy has an inner peace, they are at rest, and they have a feeling of well-being. Typically joyful people are confident, assured, and have frequent feelings of happiness. If you ask them what or how they are feeling, they will often respond, "*Great!*"

Hope placed in evil and wickedness will not end well. Trouble is on the horizon, if it has not already arrived. Problems and suffering are the typical results for making bad choices, usually the result of bad information, bad advice, or poor thinking.

Such trouble and suffering means loss, depression, mental anguish, lack of energy, and general despair. People often describe this feeling as "heartache." It can be said that this produces a broken spirit which can be debilitating because one feels lost, that no one cares, and life does not seem worthwhile. The meaning of life has been lost.

What meaning does life have for you?

"They say a person needs just three things
to be truly happy in this world:
someone to love, something to do,
and something to hope for."
Tom Bodett[68]

Three Psychiatrists

In the period leading up to WW2 there were three Jewish psychiatrists: two learned masters in the field, and one young apprentice. The first master was a man named Sigmund Freud. He had spent years studying people, striving to understand what made people tick. He had reached the conclusion that the most basic drive in the human being was the drive for pleasure. He concluded that it is our need for pleasure that explains why we do what we do, how we live.

The second master was Alfred Adler. He too spent years studying human behavior. His studies led him to disagree with Sigmund Freud. Adler was convinced that the explanation for human behavior was power. All of us grow up feeling inferior and powerless. He concluded that life was a drive to gain control, to feel we are important.

The third man was a young up-and-coming psychiatrist by the name of Victor Frankl. He hoped to follow in the footsteps of his mentors. But before his career gained any momentum WW2 started. The Nazis invaded and life became dangerous for Jews. Freud and Adler were world renowned scholars and managed to escape before Hitler invaded. Frankl was not so lucky. He was arrested and thrown into a Nazi concentration camp for four long years.

After the war was over, Frankl was released from the concentration camp and resumed his career. As he reflected upon his time as a prisoner, he realized something quite strange: the people who survived were not always the ones you'd expect. Many who were physically strong wasted away and died. Others who were seemingly physically weak survived. Why? What was it that enabled them to hang on through a living hell?

Frankl reflected on the theories of his mentors. Freud's pleasure principle couldn't explain it. For desperate and terrible years the people in that camp knew only pain, suffering and degradation. Pleasure was not a word in their vocabulary. It wasn't pleasure that kept them going.

What then of Adler's theory about power being the basic human need? That didn't hold up well either. Frankl and his fellow Jews were completely powerless during their time in the concentration camps. Each day they stared down the barrels of loaded guns, were treated like animals, and suffered jackboots on their faces. They had no power and no prospect of power.

Victor Frankl came up with his own theory. The difference between those who survived and those who perished was *hope*. Those who survived never gave up their belief that their lives had meaning, that despite everything going on around them, this period would one day end and they would again live meaningful and purposeful lives.[69]

The one thing that gives life value, that gives us purpose, is that we live with a sense of hope and that our life has meaning. If there is no meaning in life, then why bother? Life reverts to chaos where there is no purpose and hope – no meaning. Do I exist to give myself pleasure and then disappear into the mist without meaning? Does that make any sense to you? There are people who believe that nonsense. I don't I firmly believe that I exist because life does have meaning.

> *"Once you choose hope,*
> *anything's possible."*
> Christopher Reeve[70]

The Time is Now

Life goes by quickly. Elderly people looking back at their youth are particularly and poignantly aware of the passing years. The prime of life is fleeting. Thus, it is wise not to put off until tomorrow what you can do today. The time is *now*. If you do it now you won't forget about it, and won't have to worry about getting it done before some deadline. You may even be able to enjoy the fruit of your labor.

This is good advice for everyone, but particularly important for those in the prime of life. We certainly have enough freedom in life to do most of the things we want and we should and can enjoy life. Although we are often told to follow our hearts, we also need to use wisdom in making good choices.

What is Your Hope?

List the most significant "hopes" in your life? Quiet your spirit and take time to really think about what you truly hope for. What are your life hopes? What are the deep desires of your heart?

_____

_____

_____

_____

_____

_____

_____

_____

Following are some possibilities:

1. that I am right with my God.
2. that I am a faithful and loving spouse or parent.
3. that I am a faithful and true leader in my family.
4. that I am a valued friend.
5. that my children have genuine joy in life.
6. that I use my skills, gifts, and resources wisely.
7. that I am honest and true, never misleading anyone.
8. that I serve my community well.
9. that my children marry spouses who truly love them.
10. that I impact and improve someone's life.
11. that I have a life of good health.
12. that my extended family truly love one another.
13. that I will marry the love of my life.
14. that I will live to spoil my grandbabies.
15. that I will live to see my grandchildren marry.

Now go back to your list and identify the top five and prioritize them. How do your hopes fit with your Life Plan? Are they in harmony with your plans?

> *"Hope itself is like a star – not to be seen*
> *in the sunshine of prosperity, and only*
> *to be discovered in the night of adversity."*
> Charles H. Spurgeon[71]

Don't Hope in Wealth

If one or more of your hopes is in money or wealth, erase it, or cross it out. Destroy it! Hope placed in wealth fails. It is fleeting. It is fickle and it will not last. Hope in wealth comes from worldly values that disappear and can be lost forever at any time. The problem is we can tend to fall in love with money and the power it brings. Loving luxury, power, and wealth is at the root of so much trouble.

The Source of Hope

Many proverbs and wise sayings identify the source of hope as "wisdom." Wisdom is permanent. It is extremely valuable because it can guide your decisions in life. Wisdom can give us a future so we have something to look forward to (to hope in). It will not fade away like a mist after a storm. It will not vanish in the face of trouble.

Wisdom will guide us in making right decisions.

ATTITUDES AND ACTIONS THAT ENCOURAGE HOPE

- Be patient!
- Share your difficulties with a trusted friend.
- Don't be constantly critical of life.
- Focus on what's important. Give little time to the little things.
- Understand that life has challenges. Everyone experiences tough times. You are not alone in that.
- Don't live in fear. Learn and grow from difficult times. Seek understanding from life situations.
- Be kind to yourself. Celebrate victories.
- Life is a journey, not a party.
- Be content with what you have.
- Be intentional: choose hope instead of fear.

TIPS FOR BEING HOPEFUL:

- Look on the bright side. Be an optimist, not a pessimist. Be positive and encourage others.
- Have an attitude of gratitude. Be a thankful person.
- See the humor in the human condition. Laugh at yourself. Don't take life too seriously.
- Listen to <u>good</u> music, read <u>good</u> books, watch <u>good</u> movies, and have <u>good</u> friends . . . (GIGO).
- Be healthy: take care of yourself physically (sleep, food, drink, and exercise).
- Avoid bad habits: alcohol, drugs, immorality, etc.
- Live and work in positive surroundings. Minimize exposure to negative influences.
- Have a life plan. Set goals. Know where you are going. Have a sense of purpose.
- Be organized. Have a to-do list and a schedule.

"Hope is medicine for a soul
that's sick and tired."
Eric Swensson[72]

Appendix A
Self-Discipline

Results and achievement are produced
by self-discipline and self-motivation.

Self-discipline is a character trait whereby you follow a systematic process to achieve a goal. It's a personal orientation toward living life in a prescribed or regulated manner. If you have self-discipline, you approach life or problems in a systematic manner.

Many good things in life happen because we employ some form of self-discipline to achieve a desired result. Is it possible to get lucky and receive a benefit that is not really earned or deserved? Yes, but that is an exception to the way life normally happens. Self-discipline brings together the necessary components to achieve a desired outcome. This is a valuable quality for leadership.

An obvious example is an individual who wants to compete in a marathon race. Unless he is disciplined about his preparation and training, he will never be able to complete the race. This example is about running marathons, but it applies to all facets of life.

Self-discipline is a basic life skill that is needed to achieve most life goals. In the Life Planning Series we also use the term "intentionality" to represent this characteristic. It is very difficult to achieve results of any kind without self-discipline and intentionality.

IMPORTANCE OF SELF-DISCIPLINE

1. Focus
Self-discipline helps you stay focused on your goals, whether related to work, recreational activities, family, education, or other interests. When you are not focused, other work assignments can interfere with achieving your goals. It is still possible to be involved in other activities as long as you do not permit those activities to get in the way of the primary or important goal you wish to achieve.

2. Respect
Self-discipline will earn the respect of others. Disciplined work habits will create respect by co-workers and will usually be noticed by supervisors. Even those who don't practice self-discipline will admire it in others. It is easy to become a role model if you practice self-discipline. Others will come to you for help and advice. Bosses are always on the lookout for workers who are self-disciplined.

3. Self-confidence
Self-confidence is a common attitude for those who are self-disciplined. It helps a person accomplish tasks and overcome problems so both personal and work goals can be achieved efficiently. Self-discipline will produce self-confidence because goals are achieved, validating the confidence displayed.

4. Health and activity
A self-disciplined life will normally include desirable behaviors regarding diet, health, exercise, and sleep. Self-discipline will keep you focused on the important things. It will give you enthusiasm and self-confidence. Disciplined people are typically active and working toward some goal or desired result in their life or career.

5. Self-control

An undisciplined person often lacks self-control. It is much easier to get angry and give in to temptations when self-control is not present. Those without self-control will find themselves violating their core values, using hurtful words, becoming entangled in arguments, and even failing to be trustworthy.

6. Success

Passion, diligence, and hard work are all needed, along with self-discipline and intentionality to accomplish major tasks. Being self-disciplined will enable you to get work done on time, which will not be the case if you procrastinate. This leads to less stress on both home and work projects, allowing you to enjoy your work and participate in other recreational and social activities.

7. Avoid stress

There is often great stress or anxiety associated with deadlines. This is usually based on the fear of failure or worry about how your work will be accepted. Disciplining yourself to prepare well in advance of deadlines will greatly reduce the stress and tension of producing a good result. Knowing that you are well-prepared will increase your self-confidence.

CONCLUSION

Self-discipline is required in all areas of our life, especially in the home, workplace, education, and sports. It is needed in every phase of life. It is as necessary for employees serving customers at a fast-food restaurant as it is to engineers manufacturing and delivering precision-made products to NASA for the next moon mission.

Self-discipline is particularly useful in the workplace. Tasks must be done on time in every business; in some, such as healthcare facilities, time may be critical. Corporations produce products and services based on schedules, available inventory, and transportation of goods. They require self-discipline in implementing efficient work processes in order to produce, sell, and deliver quality products to the marketplace.

Appendix B
Check List

If you like to use check lists in completing tasks, we have included a check list that lists all the steps in completing the Plan.

Chapter 10: Planning Part 1 – Life Analysis, Know Yourself

☐ List the things and activities you love to do.

☐ List your greatest physical or mental skills and abilities.

☐ List your strengths, special skills, and serious passions.

☐ List your weaknesses.

☐ List any roadblocks, distractions, or hindrances that might prevent you from implementing the Leadership Life Principle.

☐ List any serious character flaws.

Chapter 11: Planning Part 2 – Life Values

☐ List your final 5 to 8 Core Values.

☐ List your top 6 to 12 Life Priorities today.

☐ How would your Life Priorities change if you knew you had only two years to live?

☐ How would the Leadership Life Principle or any new objectives change your current Life Priorities?

☐ How should the Life Analysis in Chapter 10 change your Priorities?

☐ Given the Leadership Life Principle, what new priorities would you need to adopt?

☐ Prepare a final list of your revised Life Priorities. Aim at 6 to 8, but no more than 12.

☐ List the existing traits, behaviors, activities, or habits you must manage in order to achieve the Leadership Life Principle.

☐ List your final 4 to 8 Life Commitments.

Chapter 12: Planning Part 3 – Leadership Life Principle

The Life Goal is: *I will lead well and be a loyal follower.*

Chapter 13: Planning Part 4 – Action Steps

☐ Select and list of the best 4 to 10 tips. The tips are located on pages 27, 71, 88, 106, 118, 129, 139, and 145.

☐ Choose the top 4 to 6 tips and list them in priority order.

☐ Choose and list the implementation techniques that would be helpful to you in implementing your plan.

☐ Produce and list your initial list of actions steps for making the Leadership Life Principle a reality in your life.

☐ Cull and consolidate the initial list.

☐ List action steps for those situations that will make your commitment to the Leadership Life Principle difficult to achieve.

☐ List the existing personal characteristics that must be improved to achieve your objectives.

☐ List the core values, priorities, or commitments that require action steps in order to achieve the Leadership Life Principle.

☐ List the 2 to 6 "Tips For Improvement" that you feel would be particularly effective for you.

☐ Reduce the working list to only the good and workable ideas. Eliminate or combine the duplicates.

☐ Identify and list the helpful "TECHNIQUES FOR IMPLEMENTATION" that warrant inclusion in your action steps.

☐ List action steps relative to what you will do if something fails.

☐ Cull and consolidate the list.

☐ Prioritize the groups and the individual actions within groups.

☐ FINAL ACTION STEPS: Choose the 4 to 6 best action steps from your list.

☐ TECHNOLOGY: Consider entering information or reminders on your phone, tablet, or computer.

☐ REVIEW:
   a) Are your action steps consistent with your core values and revised life priorities?
   b) Are your action steps consistent with your personal desires and commitments?

☐ Modify your plans as necessary.

Chapter 14: Planning Part 5 – Ongoing Progress Review

☐ During the first eight weeks, review your plans weekly.

☐ Review your plan for success and failure. Make necessary changes.

☐ Modify and update your plan as needed.

Transformation Roadmap

Wisdom That Transforms!

1. True leadership is measured by one's ability to inspire action toward shared goals through trust and service, not titles or charisma.

2. Prioritizing others' growth and organizational well-being over self-interest builds sustainable success and aligns with your moral integrity.

3. Leadership principles anchor personal and organizational integrity. Working consistent to your core values like accountability, service, and ethical behavior ensures alignment between your actions and your aspirations for the organization.

4. Leadership is a universal responsibility. Everyone, regardless of role, influences others through their choices; embracing this mindset elevates daily interactions and drives collective progress toward meaningful goals.

Twelve Principles of Leadership

#1 Communication: Effective communication is essential for effective leadership.

#2 Training and Development: Effective leaders prioritize continuous training and development for themselves and their teams.

#3 Decision Making: Effective leaders are decisive, confident in their decision-making process, and skilled at problem-solving.

#4 Core Values: Leaders must embody and uphold strong core values that guide their actions, decisions, and moral standards, setting the tone for the entire team or organization.

#5 Managing Change: Good leaders embrace change by recognizing its inevitability and potential benefits, adapting quickly to new circumstances and technologies, fostering a culture of innovation and curiosity within their teams.

#6 Lead By Example: Leading by example means that leaders inspire followers by actively participating in the work themselves, demonstrating diligence and modeling the desired behaviors and values.

#7 Teamwork:
Effective teamwork is fostered by leaders who promote cooperation, open communication, and a shared sense of purpose among team members.

#8 Ownership and Responsibility: Effective leaders embrace a mindset of ownership and responsibility, proactively addressing problems, taking accountability for team outcomes, and fostering a culture where every member feels responsible for the organization's success.

#9 Planning: Organized leaders prioritize planning as a fundamental responsibility, ensuring clear objectives, well-defined action plans, and consistent communication.

#10 Delegation: Good delegation involves entrusting responsibility and authority to capable individuals, fostering their growth, and optimizing team performance.

#11 Following Leaders: Effective leaders must also be good followers, demonstrating respect and clear communication with their superiors while supporting organizational goals.

#12 Motivation: Effective leaders create a motivating and inspiring environment by connecting with their team on a personal level, harnessing emotions to drive positive results, and providing a clear vision and purpose that makes every individual feel valued and committed.

5. Leadership is rooted in continuous growth. Cultivating skills like effective communication, problem-solving, and adaptability ensures you can navigate challenges and inspire others.

6. Honesty and integrity are non-negotiable. Living by unwavering honesty, truth, and moral principles ensures long-term success and self-respect, even when faced with external pressures or temptations.

7. Leading with transparency and responsibility creates a ripple effect, inspiring trust and ethical behavior in others while fostering a legacy of dignity and fairness.

8. Surround yourself with excellence. Hiring and empowering people who challenge or surpass your skills amplifies collective success, fostering growth for both the team and your own leadership legacy.

9. Staying committed to core goals and making tough, customer-centric decisions.

10. Recognize team strengths. Celebrate collaboration.

11. Embracing change while honoring past achievements and staying mission-driven ensures resilience, keeping your actions anchored to meaningful goals beyond ego.

12. Embracing calculated risks and learning from mistakes fosters resilience, turning decisions into stepping stones rather than obstacles.

Your decisions shape your life.
Start building with intention!

Free PDF
Life Improvement Principles
[Get the ebook version for 99 cents]

You can live your best life!

Welcome to a journey of discovery! In case you have forgotten, your actions have consequences. Unlock your potential! This book (60+ pages) provides the overview of all our strategies and wisdom principles to live your best life. You *can* transform your life! Get your wisdom-based roadmap to a better life and unlock all the possibilities for growth and success.

Free PDF: https://getwisdompublishing.com/resource-registration/

Kindle ebook for 99 cents:
https://www.amazon.com/dp/B0FG883KZM

Ebook

Free PDF

Make it your life goal to be the best you can be!

Discover Wisdom and live the life you deserve.

Your Next Steps

Change Your Life with purpose and intention!

Should you read other books in this series?

We recommend that if you acquire any books in the Series, you should also obtain *CHOOSE Integrity*. This is the foundational book in the series. We also believe the four books covering the other Primary Life Principles would be particularly useful for living a better life: Friends, Speech, Diligence (Work), and Money.

CHOOSE Faith

This is a unique book in the Series. It addresses all the important spiritual type questions you might consider. It answers questions like: Does God exist? Why should I care about faith? What's religion all about? Does eternal life really exist? I don't know the right questions to ask. What is the truth? This book will help you find answers to your spiritual questions.

LIFE PLANNING HANDBOOK

This book is also unique. If you are interested in doing a complete life plan that covers all aspects of your life, not just a specific topic like those addressed in The Life Planning Series, go to:

https://www.amazon.com/dp/1952359325

You can live a better life.
Just Decide You Want to!

The Life Planning Series
These books can improve your life.

LIFE PLANNING HANDBOOK	A Life Plan will shape your life journey! The next step in your life planning.
CHOOSE INTEGRITY	Life Principle: Be honest, live with integrity, and base your life on truth.
CHOOSE FRIENDS WISELY	Life Principle: Choose your friends wisely.
CHOOSE THE RIGHT WORDS	Life Principle: Guard your speech.
CHOOSE GOOD WORK HABITS	Life Principle: Be diligent and a hard worker.
CHOOSE FINANCIAL RESPONSIBILITY	Life Principle: Make sound financial choices.

CHOOSE A POSITIVE SELF-IMAGE	**Life Principle:** Be confident in who you are.
CHOOSE LEADERSHIP	**Life Principle:** Lead well and be a loyal follower.
CHOOSE CORE VALUES	**Life Principle:** Core values will drive your life.
CHOOSE LOVE AND FAMILY	**Life Principle:** Build strong relationships.
CHOOSE FAITH	*Your Spiritual Guidebook for Questions about Religion, God, Heaven, Truth, Evil, and the Afterlife.*

Go to: **https://www.amazon.com/dp/B09TH9SYC4**

to get your copy.

Create a life based on purpose, meaning, and lasting fulfillment.

Acknowledgments

My wife has patiently persevered while I indulged my interest in this subject. Thank you for your patience.

Our older daughter has been an invaluable resource. She has also graciously produced our website at www.lifeplanningtools.com

Our middle daughter designed all the covers for this series. We are very grateful for her help, talent and creativity.

Notes

QUOTES

ACCURACY: We have used a number of quotes throughout this book that came from our files, notes, books, public articles, the Internet, etc. We have made no attempt to verify that these quotes were actually written or spoken by the person they are attributed to. Regardless of the source of these quotes, the wisdom of the underlying message is relative to the content in this book and worth noting, even if the source reference is erroneous.

SOURCE: Unless otherwise specifically noted below the quotes used herein can be sourced from a number of different websites on the Internet that provide lists of quotes by subject or author. The same or similar quotes will appear on multiple sites. Therefore, rather than assign individual quote sources, we are providing a list of sites where we might have found the quotes that were used in this book:

--azquotes.com
--brainyquote.com
--codeofliving.com
--everydaypower.com
--goodhousekeeping.com
--goodreads.com/quotes
--graciousquotes.com
--inc.com
--keepinspiring.me
--notable-quotes.com
--parade.com
--plantetofsuccess.com
--quotemaster.org
--quotir.com
--success.com
--thoughtco.com
--thoughtcatalog.com
--wisdomquotes.com
--wisesayings.com
--wow4u.com

1 Jack Ma, see QUOTES above.
2 Stephen H Berkey, www.amazon.com/author/stephenhberkey.
3 Latin American saying, see QUOTES above.
4 Aesop, see QUOTES above.
5 SermonCentral.com; contributed by Perry Greene

6 --

7 --

8 --

9 Roger Crawford, see QUOTES above.

10 Cicero, see QUOTES above.

11 John Maxwell, see QUOTES above.

12 Unknown, https://www.qualtrics.com/blog/10-powerful-leadership-quotes/

13 Jim Rohn, https://www.qualtrics.com/blog/10-powerful-leadership-quotes/

14 John Maxwell, https://www.qualtrics.com/blog/10-powerful-leadership-quotes/

15 John Quincy Adams, see QUOTES above.

16 Madeleine Albright, see QUOTES above.

17 John F. Kennedy, see QUOTES above.

18 Steve Jobs, see QUOTES above.

19 Sukant Ratnakar, see QUOTES above.

20 Bill Gates, see QUOTES above.

21 --

22 Ralph Waldo Emerson, see QUOTES above.

23 --

24 Rosalynn Carter, see QUOTES above.

25 Jesse Jackson, see QUOTES above.

26 Theodore M. Hesburgh, see QUOTES above.

27 Napoleon Hill, see QUOTES above.

28 John C. Maxwell, see QUOTES above.

29 Reed Markham, see QUOTES above.

30 Earl Weaver, see QUOTES above.

31 - - -

32 Bob Proctor, see QUOTES above.

33 Oprah Winfrey, see QUOTES above.

34 Study by the UK Institute of Business Ethics, https://stu.edu/news/answers-for-seekers-what-is-ethical-leadership/

35 Martin Luther King, Jr., see QUOTES above.

36 John Quincy Adams, see QUOTES above.

37 Steve Jobs, see QUOTES above.

38 Warren G. Bennis, see QUOTES above.

39 Zig Ziglar, see QUOTES above.

40 T.S. Eliot, see QUOTES above.

41 Dolly Parton, see QUOTES above.

42 Kenneth Blanchard, see QUOTES above.

43 Les Brown, see QUOTES above.

44 Brian Tracy, see QUOTES above.

45 Socrates, see QUOTES above.

46 Bob Proctor, see QUOTES above.

47 Walter Cronkite, see QUOTES above.

48-65 -none-

66 Barbara Kingsolver. *Animal Dreams*, Harper Perennial; Reissue edition (2013), ISBN-13: 978-0062278500.

67 Glenn van Dekken, see QUOTES above.

68 Tom Bodett, see QUOTES above.

69 Victor Frankl, Based on a talk given by Australian speaker Michael Frost.

70 Christopher Reeve, see QUOTES above.

71 Charles H. Spurgeon, see QUOTES above.

72 Eric Swensson, see QUOTES above.

General Sources:

1. 11 principles of leadership, https://www.wgu.edu/blog/11-principles-leadership2006.html#close.

2. THE 10 MOST IMPORTANT PRINCIPLES OF LEADERSHIP, DAVIS M.J. AURINI JANUARY 9, 2014.

3. 25 Leadership Qualities That Makes You A Good Leader, Anjan Pathak Leaderhttps://blog.vantagecircle.com/tag/leadership/, Updated on 28 July 2022

4. Eight Leadership techniques every leader should know https://focus3.com/leadership-skills-8-principles-every-leader-should-know/

5. Seven Leadership Principles Every Leader Needs To Understand, Leadership Strategies Leadership Development, Jason Diamond Arnold, January 18, 2019

6. Twelve Principles of Leadership, Alex Czartoryski   May 15, 2017, Twelve key principles of leadership, taken from the book "Extreme Ownership," Willink and Babin.

7. Leadership Principles, https://www.bezosacademy.org/leadership-principles/

8. Ten Leadership Principles for Next Generation Leaders, COLIN BAKER   Feb 2, 2022

9. Fourteen Amazon Leadership Principles and Why They Matter, https://leaders.com/leadership/

10. What is Ethical Leadership? Principles & Examples, Barry D. Moore, Jan 17, 2022

11. Leadership Effectiveness: How to be a Better Leader; https://www.gallup.com/cliftonstrengths/en/356072/how-to-be-better-leader.

12. 10 Awesome Tips for Being a Better Leader, By Carly Okyle October 21, 2014 https://www.entrepreneur.com/leadership.

13. Eighteen tips for effective leadership, https://www.indeed.com/career-advice/career-development/

14. 20 Leadership Experts Share Their Best Leadership Tips, John Brandon, Contributing editor, https://www.inc.com/john-brandon/20-leadership-experts-share-their-best-leadership-tip.html.

15. Twenty Qualities of a Great Leader (with Tips), Erin Wike, Updated November 29, 2021 | Published January 30, 2019.

16. The Best Yes, Lysa Terkeurst, Publisher: Nelson Books, ISBN 978-1-4002-0585-1.

17. YES or NO, Jeff Shinabarger, Publisher: David C Cook (2014), ISBN 979-0781408219.

18 Your Blueprint for LIFE, Michael Kendrick, Publisher: Nelson Books, ISBN 978-1-40002-0660-5.

About the Author

The author graduated from the Business School at Indiana University and obtained a master's degree at Georgia State University in Atlanta. His first career was as a senior executive with a top insurance and financial institution, where he spent a number of years directing strategic planning for one of their major divisions.

In the 1990s he founded an online Internet business which he sold in 2010. He began to write and publish books and materials that led to an interest in personal life planning. This resulted in combining the wisdom of wise sayings and proverbs with life planning and the result is the Life Planning Series and the Life Planning Handbook.

The author, his wife, and two of his children and their families live in the Nashville, TN area.

WEBSITE: http://www.lifeplanningtools.com

AMAZON: www.amazon.com/author/jswellman

Contact Us

	www.lifeplanningtools.com info@lifeplanningtools.com	Website Email
Facebook	JSWellman	
	www.amazon.com/author/jswellman	**Author Page**
Life Planning Series	www.amazon.com/dp/B09TH9SYC4	
	www.lifeplanningtools.link/newsletter	**Monthly News Letter**

You can help

IDEAS and SUGGESTIONS: If you have a suggestion to improve this book, please let us know.

Mention our LIFE PLANNING books on your social platforms and recommend them to your family and friends.

Thank you!

Make a Difference

"The law of prosperity is generosity.
If you want more, give more."
Bob Proctor[57]

Have you ever done something just out of kindness or goodwill without wanting or expecting anything in return? I'm going to ask you to do <u>two things</u> just for that reason. The first will be just out of the goodness of your heart and the second to make an impact in someone else's life.

It won't cost you anything and it won't take a lot of time or effort.

This Book

First, what did you think of this book? Give the book an honest review in order for us to compete with the giant publishers. What did you like and how did it impact you? It will only take you several minutes to leave your review at: **https://www.amazon.com/dp/1952359457**

Follow the link above to the Amazon sales page, scroll down about three quarters of the page and click the box that says: "Write a customer review." It does not have to be long or well-written – just tell other readers what you think about the book. Or, just score the book on a scale of 1 – 5 stars (5 is high).

This will help us a great deal and we so appreciate your willingness to help. If you want to tell us something about

the book directly, you can email us at:
info@lifeplanningtools.com.

Give Books to Students and Employees

Secondly, do you know any schools or organizations that might want to give this book or our Life Planning Handbook to their students or emloyees?

Here is how you can help. If you send us the contact information and allow us to use your name, we will contact the person or persons you suggest with all the details. Obviously there would be special pricing and if the order is large enough, a message from the organization's CEO could be included on the printed pages.

Alternatively, you can personally give a copy of one of our books to the organization for their consideration. We would recommend our Life Planning Handbook, but some organizations might be interested in a specific subject. If they are interested in this partnership with us, they should contact us directly.

It is not that difficult to help someone live a better life: just a little time and intentionality. Let us hear from you if you want to make a difference in someone's life!

J. S. Wellman
Extra-mile Publishing
steve@lifeplanningtools.com
www.lifeplanningtools.com

Wisdom Without Action is Just information

LIFE PLANNING SERIES
J.S. WELLMAN

www.ingramcontent.com/pod-product-compliance
Lightning Source LLC
Chambersburg PA
CBHW060012050426
42448CB00012B/2716